Linking Up and Reaching Out in Bangladesh

Linking Up and Reaching Out in Bangladesh

Information and Communications Technology for Microfinance

Henry K. Bagazonzya, Zaid Safdar,
A.K.M. Abdullah, Cecile Thioro Niang, and
Aneeka Rahman

THE WORLD BANK
Washington, D.C.

ISBN: 978-0-8213-8175-5
eISBN: 978-0-8213-8176-2
DOI: 10.1596/978-0-8213-8175-5

Cover design by Quantum Think

Cataloging-in-publication data has been requested.

Contents

Figures

Tables

Acknowledgments

This book was prepared by a team led by Henry Bagazonzya and A. K. M. Abdullah as co-task team leaders, Zaid Safdar, Thyra Riley, Cecile Thioro Niang, Aneeka Rahman, Luis de la Vega (consultant), and Saleh Khan (consultant). The team wishes to acknowledge the support provided by Bridget Rosario Rosalind and Aza Rashid throughout the study and Sashikala Krishani Teyaraj for the final formatting of the draft report. The team also wishes to thank the peer reviewers: Gautam Ivatury Consultive Group to Assist the Poorest (CGAP); Samuel Munzele Maimbo; and Rizza Maniego-Eala, President of G-Xchange, Inc., in the Philippines, whose comments on the concept note focused the team's study objectives. The team is grateful for insightful comments from Gautam Ivatury, Samuel Munzele Maimbo, Greg Chen (CGAP in South Asia), Shamsuddin Ahmad, and Shanila Azher (U.K. Department for International Development) on the draft text of the book, and invaluable comments regarding next steps in the process of creating and implementing a centralized ICT platform for the microfinance industry. A section responding to these comments is included in the introduction. The team greatly appreciates the overall project guidance and support provided by Simon Bell (Sector Manager).

Abbreviations

3G	Third generation
ACH	Automated clearinghouse
AML	Anti–money laundering
ASP	Application service provider
ATM	Automated teller machine
BRAC	Bangladesh Rural Advancement Committee
BTCL	Bangladesh Telecommunications Company Limited
BTRC	Bangladesh Telecommunication Regulatory Commission
BTTB	Bangladesh Telegraph and Telephone Board
CBS	Core Banking System
CDF	Credit and Development Forum
CEO	Chief executive officer
CGAP	Consultative Group to Assist the Poor
CIB	Credit Information Bureau
CICA	Controller of ICT Certifying Authorities
DFID	Department for International Development (United Kingdom)
DIS	Deposit Insurance Scheme
DSL	Digital subscriber line
EFTPOS	Electronic funds transfer at point of sale

FINO	Financial Information Network & Operations Ltd
GDP	Gross domestic product
HCC	Hosted call center
ICT	Information and communication technology
ICX	Interconnection exchange
IFC	International Finance Corporation
IGW	International gateway
ILDTS	International Long Distance Telecommunications Services
IMF	International Monetary Fund
INAFI	International Network of Alternative Financial Institutions
IT	Information technology
IX	Internet exchange
MFI	Microfinance institution
MIS	Management information system
MLP	Microcredit linkage program
MIX	Microfinance Information Exchange
MRA	Microcredit Regulatory Authority
MRRU	Microfinance Research and Reference Unit
NGO	Nongovernmental organization
NSC	National Steering Committee
PKSF	Palli Karma-Sahayak Foundation
POS	Point of sale
PPP	Public-private partnership
PSTN	Public switched telephone network
RSI	Rural Servicios Informáticos
SaaS	Software as a service
SDC	Swiss Agency for Development and Cooperation
SME	Small and medium enterprise
SWIFT	Society for Worldwide Interbank Financial Telecommunication
TMSS	Thengamara Mohila Sabuj Shangha
UN	United Nations
VoIP	Voice-over-Internet protocol
WiMAX	Worldwide Interoperability for Microwave Access

CHAPTER 1

Introduction

The microfinance market in Bangladesh emerged in the early 1970s out of the now-famous Jobra experiments of Dr. Muhammad Yunus and a number of other, government-led initiatives. These pioneering efforts led to the proliferation of institutions that we see flourishing in the country today. Bangladesh is generally considered to be a mature microfinance market, with a multitude of players that together employ around 150,000 people (CDF 2006).

According to data provided by the Microcredit Regulatory Authority (MRA), as of December 7, 2008, there were 374 licensed nongovernmental microfinance organizations in Bangladesh—out of 4,236 organizations that applied for licenses. The potential number that could qualify, given the major criteria of having 1,000 borrowers or Tk 4 million in principal loans outstanding, is 452. Data from MIX, the Web-based microfinance information platform (Microfinance Information Exchange) and Credit and Development Forum (CDF), a nonprofit microfinance network in Bangladesh, indicate that 77 percent of the market is currently served by the three largest microcredit programs: ASA, Bangladesh Rural Advancement Committee (BRAC), and Grameen Bank. Together, the three institutions serve more than 18 million borrowers. The remainder of Bangladesh's estimated 24 million total microfinance borrowers are served by institutions classified as medium, small, or very small.

While the figures seem to indicate that large institutions serve the vast majority of microfinance clients in Bangladesh, a mapping exercise carried out by the microfinance apex funding institution Palli Karma-Sahayak Foundation (PKSF) found that there is an overlap of about 33 percent (PKSF 2004). More recent PKSF studies indicate that the overlap rate has increased to 40 percent. In other words, borrowers receive loans from multiple lenders, either to fulfill their investment needs or to pay back the loans they have received from other institutions. Given the overlap incidence and the absence of a robust credit bureau, totals on an institution-by-institution basis might grossly overestimate the number of borrowers served and therefore underestimate those that have absolutely no access to finance. This leads to what is widely believed: that despite the large number of (sometimes duplicated) borrowers currently served and despite the many years of experience in microfinance by the Bangladeshi operators, about 50 percent of the country's poor have not yet been reached (PKSF 2006). Although microfinance organizations in Bangladesh do not yet see this as a problem, it has become a troublesome issue in many other counties, as it can lead to unacceptable levels of debt that would eventually adversely affect the poor. The 2008–09 international financial crisis provides incentive for Bangladesh to be cautious about such an occurrence in its microfinance sector.

Current Constraints in the Microfinance Industry

Microcredit organizations in Bangladesh face a number of constraints in trying to serve the majority of the poor. Many of these constraints can be linked to insufficient availability and use of technology. Major concerns include the following:

- There is no reporting mechanism that correctly captures performance data. Information on the financial and operational performance of microfinance institutions (MFIs) is paper-centric and not timely, while data are not complete and cannot be independently verified. This situation is detrimental to MFIs, microfinance clients, and microfinance industry regulatory bodies.
- Paper-based operations consume a significant amount of loan officers' time.

- There is not, in most MFIs, a timely connection between the head office, the branch offices, and the loan officers in the field due to lack of, or incomplete use of, appropriate technology applications.
- Due to non-use of appropriate technology applications, there is a lack of holistic, sector-wide data on MFI borrowers and outstanding portfolios. MFIs are unable to share useful information about clients with each other. This contributes to the persistent client overlap seen in the microfinance sector.
- Adoption of technology is expensive for MFIs, while use of currently-available technology does not always correspond to gains in revenue or increases in productivity in the short term.
- Capitalization of MFIs is hampered by the lack of a transparent reporting mechanism that could help potential funders to quickly understand the financial health and transparency of MFIs seeking funding. It takes too long for potential investors to collect, collate, and analyze data, which leads investors to work with only a few MFIs—those that can provide ready-to-use or near-ready-to-use data and information.
- Launching new product lines such as branchless banking applications requires an advanced level of technology usage beyond an enabling environment. The fact that most MFIs in Bangladesh have not reached such a level means that they will find it difficult to take full advantage of branchless banking, remittance services, or other cost-effective mechanisms of reaching rural and poor people with demand-driven financial products.
- The fact that MFIs are not able to take advantage of many technology-based initiatives means that they are not able to reap the benefits of new services provided by the private sector, including from Information Technology (IT) vendors, telecom companies, or of public sector programs, such as safety net payment arrangements.

From this list, it is clear that MFIs in Bangladesh use technology in an ad hoc fashion and go only partway in automating their operations. Many interventions have been put into place, to provide funding to the poorest of the poor. PKSF has, with its partner organizations, been at the forefront of such efforts through the help of the World Bank. Other institutions are also implementing the methodology, but there remain a large number of very poor people who have no appropriate access to these institutional funding arrangements. Increased use of technology would help modernize Bangladesh's microfinance industry and enable MFIs to offer new products and services to a larger number of clients.

The Proposed New Microfinance Paradigm

This book presents a new paradigm for introducing technology in the microfinance industry of Bangladesh that could help ameliorate current constraints. Under the new paradigm, a centralized ICT platform would be established to serve the microfinance industry of Bangladesh and technology would be deployed more rapidly to MFIs in all parts of the microfinance value chain, from the head office to branch offices, loan officers, and clients. Unlike in the traditional paradigm, the technology needs of all MFIs would be pooled together in one central office. The central office would offer technology tools, services, and know-how to MFIs throughout the country. Several benefits would be achieved under this new paradigm:

- Because all technology needs would be pooled in one place, the central office would be able to exploit economies of scale and offer technology services to MFIs at a lower cost.
- Because their technology needs would be outsourced, MFI staff would no longer need to devote as much time and effort to learning new technologies. The central office would provide all technology-related training and support.
- Because technology would be deployed throughout the microfinance value chain, all parts of the MFI would always be connected.
- Because all MFIs would be connected with one another through a central office, they would be able to learn useful information about clients from one another.

The new paradigm goes several steps further. If the central platform were connected to the formal financial sector, MFI activities could become integrated with those of the formal financial sector, namely through increasing MFIs' access to capital from commercial banks and financial intermediaries. In turn, the formal financial market would be able to reach out to individual MFIs and their clients who live in remote, rural areas. Similarly, if the central platform were connected with the government, MFIs could more easily comply with government regulations and grant the government access to selected MFI information. In turn, the government could design better-targeted microfinance policies and regulations based on complete and accurate information. In the long term, the government could opt for lighter regulation, intervening strategically only when there is a need. With the new platform in place, the cost of regulation would also be lower than in the traditional paradigm, since information about MFIs would be readily available and interventions would be more strategic.

Introduction of the centralized ICT platform also would open the door to new products and services, such as mobile banking, branchless banking, and electronic remittances. Because MFIs would transact business electronically, through the central office, they would be able to store information and offer services electronically. Offering clients financial services over mobile phones would expand MFIs' outreach by allowing them to exploit the full breadth of the national mobile network. By providing their loan officers with electronic devices, MFIs would gain the ability to provide a full range of financial services otherwise available only at a branch office. Since the entire microfinance value chain would be managed electronically under the new paradigm, remittances would also be channeled electronically, enabling clients to send money to (and receive money from) a person who is a client of another MFI.

Approach to and Methodology behind the Study on Development of a Centralized ICT Platform

The hypothesis for this study is that a centralized ICT platform is good for the microfinance sector in Bangladesh and that its benefits could be achieved effectively only if (1) there were a supportive legal and regulatory framework, and (2) demand for cost-effective applications could reduce costs and facilitate outreach to remote and rural areas with demand-driven financial products. In order to test this hypothesis, the team set out to look at the state of microfinance in Bangladesh, to determine whether the legal and regulatory environment was supportive (without delving into diagnostic details), and to determine which applications would appreciably increase outreach of financial services in rural Bangladesh, given the circumstances on the ground and the international experience. The team also looked at the availability of local vendors that could support a technology platform. The information and analysis in this book were obtained through interviews with practitioners and other stakeholders across the microfinance sector in Bangladesh. Discussions were held with officials from financial sector regulators, microfinance regulators, telecom regulators, the apex microfinance organization and networks, MFIs, telecom providers, software providers, and a range of other constituents.

Several in-country visits were conducted and a thorough literature search was done on the microfinance and financial sectors of Bangladesh, drawing from existing publications and data from institutions such as the Consultative Group to Assist the Poorest (CGAP), CDF, the United Kingdom's DFID, International Finance Corporation (IFC), the International Network of Alternative Financial Institutions (INAFI), the Institute of Microfinance (in Bangladesh), the MIX, PKSF, and the World Bank. This information was used to identify key stakeholders across the industry and the pertinent challenges to the development of the sector. In addition, the team preparing the book drew upon the technology and expertise of CGAP and others in the broader microfinance industry to obtain information about global best practices and lessons learned.

The first country visit established a list of key stakeholders in ICT and microfinance. Interviews and meetings were conducted with these stakeholders using structured questionnaires and discussion checklists to gather data and conduct preliminary analysis. Subsequently, several one-on-one meetings and workshops were held to rally the support of microfinance stakeholders and the formal financial sector in the adoption of ICT in the microfinance industry. Finally, in November 2008, the team held final consultative meetings with the stakeholders, including representatives from DFID, IFC, and other donor organizations, to ensure that the findings were applicable to the current state of the microfinance industry in Bangladesh and that there was buy-in from the stakeholders.

Recommendations of the Study

The study recommends that a centralized ICT platform be established. Such an arrangement would provide benefits to microcredit organizations, the private sector, and public sector stakeholders, while clients would also obtain access to more robust financial and nonfinancial products. The cost of establishing this platform, given simplified assumptions of the number of microcredit organizations, branch and regional offices, and loan officers and the size of the overall industry loan portfolio, is estimated to be $26.18 million. Of the total cost, $8.78 million is needed during the first three years and $17.40 million during the second three years. The break-even point will be reached after six years of operation. The financial plan shows $87.15 million would be recovered during the last three years. These costs would be more accurately determined as part of the business plan for the platform.

As shown in the remainder of this book, the centralized ICT platform would exploit economies of scale. It would provide benefits to all participating stakeholders and would be financially viable when it caters to the entire microfinance market of Bangladesh. The large financial recovery during the last three years indicates that the host institution would be capable of recovering its initial investment if it sustains its operations over the long run. In order to further demonstrate the viability of the platform, a sensitivity analysis testing changes in certain important parameters was carried out as part of the study. The analysis included slower-than-expected implementation phasing, lower ICT expenses for MFIs during early years than in later years, higher-than-expected per-unit costs of setting up the platform by the host institution, and slower-than-expected loan portfolio growth. The analysis revealed that the viability of the platform was sensitive only to slower-than-expected loan portfolio growth. Other parameters affect the eventual income flows and the initial investment amounts but do not affect the viability of the ICT platform.

An analysis of the enabling environment indicates that no microfinance, financial sector, or ICT regulations would prevent the operationalization of the proposed centralized ICT platform. Going forward, the regulatory space would benefit from further embracing and facilitating new financial sector infrastructure through the platform, with the aim of achieving universal access to formal finance in Bangladesh. Recent technology license developments open promising developments for financial services applications to reach the poor. Regulatory areas that could be addressed to leverage the platform include nonbank payment systems, consumer protection regulations, and strengthening the efficiency of microfinance regulatory oversight.

Development and implementation of the centralized ICT platform would require an appropriate governance structure to ensure that the MFIs and other stakeholders are fully engaged. In this regard, the study team considered several institutional models, including a public sector model, a private sector model, and a public-private partnership model (PPP). The report recommends that a PPP[1] fulfilling the following basic design principles be put in place:

- The agency should be respected by all the participants and stakeholders in order to ensure trust in the data of the participating MFIs being held in confidence;

- The agency should be a neutral player, independent of any financial institution, government agency, or technology vendor, and should be focused on the whole microfinance industry rather than institutional goals;
- The agency should be representative by encouraging all players in the microfinance market to participate, irrespective of size;
- The agency must demonstrate the capacity to manage both the participants and the technology to be introduced;
- The agency must have a business plan that will lead to financial sustainability; and
- The agency must be efficient, financially accountable, and transparent, and it must not be in violation of any legal or regulatory framework.

Finally, next steps in establishing the platform include a comprehensive business plan containing the following:

- An update on various organizations involved in the provision of microcredit in Bangladesh, including those run by government;
- Detailed cost projections and a financial plan with robust assumptions;
- Technical and operational designs of the platform including use of off-the-shelf technology solutions to be procured from either international or local vendors; and
- Proposed funding arrangements and policy-making and capacity-building assistance that government agencies may require, including implementation arrangements and determination of the host institution.

Ultimately, the centralized ICT platform could be expected to bring about several positive transformations within the microfinance sector in Bangladesh—cost reduction, increased efficiency, broader range of MFI product offerings, better integration of microfinance into the formal financial sector, and faster growth of the microfinance market.

Note

1. Crafting an appropriate partnership to manage the entity will be a challenge. It is therefore important that institutions that will be part of this arrangement realize from the beginning that the PPP must fulfill the requirements laid out here if the entity is to serve its purpose.

CHAPTER 2

Bangladesh Microfinance Market Overview

This chapter reviews the current state of the microfinance sector in Bangladesh. It identifies the key stakeholders, describes the different market players, and describes the financial and nonfinancial products that they offer. It also looks at the potential this market provides for the use of technology for new product development and opportunities for linking the microfinance sector to the formal financial system. The primary purpose of the chapter is to provide an analysis of the key challenges facing the growth, sustainability, and outreach of microfinance services.

Country Overview: Bangladesh[1]

The growth and overall economic performance of Bangladesh have historically been challenged by its ever-increasing population. The country has the highest population density in the world—1,198 people per square kilometer in 2006, compared to 86 people per square kilometer in low-income countries, 313 people per square kilometer in countries within South Asia, and 50 people per square kilometer for the world as a whole. Bangladesh's true population figure is believed to be even higher than the 141.8 million reported by the government in 2006. International Monetary Fund (IMF) estimates put it at 156 million in 2006, giving the country a population density of 1,057 per square kilometer. The medium-variant forecast by the United Nations (UN) projects that the population of Bangladesh will reach 218 million by 2030.

This rapid population growth, however, could be reversed with the right mix of policy interventions and human capacity development. At a time when the working-age population of most countries is shrinking, the working-age proportion of the population in Bangladesh is forecast to rise substantially. This has the potential to translate into higher employment, savings and investment, and—ultimately—higher economic growth.

In view of the ever-increasing population density and consequent urbanization in Bangladesh, policy makers face two challenges: poverty reduction and job creation. About 40 percent of the population lives below the $1-per-day poverty line. This figure was revised in 2008 to $1.25 per day in light of improved data on cost of living PPPs from the International Comparison Program and new household surveys. The two challenges become even more pressing during the times of natural disaster, such as floods and cyclones, which are not uncommon in Bangladesh.

Bangladesh's macroeconomic performance in recent years has been remarkably resilient to multiple natural disasters and elevated international food and fuel prices. In 2006, the gross domestic product (GDP) per capita (purchasing power parity adjusted) stood at $1,230, compared to $1,860 for low-income countries as a whole and $2,289 for South Asian countries. GDP growth was 6.6 percent for the same year, compared to 8 percent for low-income countries and 8.6 percent for South Asia. Real GDP growth is expected to average 6.1 percent per year in 2008–12, the same as in 2003–07. For fiscal year 2009, GDP growth is expected to be between 4.8 and 5.6 percent. The main risk associated with this GDP growth historically has been Bangladesh's dependence on imports of oil and food. This, however, is not a major threat at the moment, given the sharp decline in oil and food prices as a result of the global recession following the financial crisis.

The other main area of weakness concerning GDP growth in Bangladesh is the country's dependence on garment exports and remittances for foreign exchange. Ready-made garment exports account for about 75 percent of export earnings. In the face of the decline in consumer spending in developed countries following the crisis, Bangladesh's main export revenues are under threat. Recent data show that remittances are also decreasing. These factors indicate likely pressure on the current account balance.

On a positive note, the relative nonintegration of Bangladesh's financial markets with those in the rest of the world has insulated the country against the global slowdown. The foreign exchange reserves of the Bangladesh Bank (the country's central bank) and commercial banks have limited exposure to the securities markets in the United States and the European Union. But while nonintegration of financial markets in Bangladesh with the global market appears to have benefited the country during the crisis, nonintegration has stunted the growth of the country as well.

On the domestic front, commodity prices in Bangladesh have been a major issue for the past several years. The government's efforts to curb increases in imported food prices were not successful until the global oil and commodity markets experienced a downturn brought on by the financial crisis. Unless domestic crop output is hit by natural disaster, it is likely that food prices will decrease further—or at least remain stable—in the next year. Thus, the IMF has indicated that the threat to growth resulting from increasing inflationary pressures will be less over the next six months to one year (IMF 2008).

Bangladesh's financial sector is dominated by commercial banks, which collectively hold assets of 53 percent of GDP. The market capitalization of listed companies is about 6 percent of GDP. In addition to the four state-owned commercial banks, the country's 43 commercial banks in 2007 included 30 private banks and 9 foreign banks.

Though the spread between lending and deposit rates in Bangladesh typically has been more than 500 basis points, a new directive issued to the main commercial banks should have resulted in a slight reduction in the lending rate during the course of 2008 (figure 2.1). The IMF estimates

Figure 2.1   Interest Rates

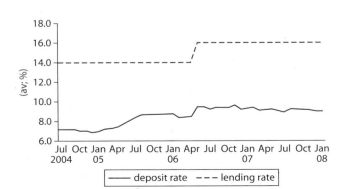

Source: EIU 2008.

that successful financial sector development is the keystone to securing the future growth potential of Bangladesh, and that while the banking sector is growing, the state-owned commercial banks still undermine the efficiency of the system (IMF 2008).

Inflation in Bangladesh is expected to fall from 2009 onward, as a sustained recovery in the agricultural sector boosts food stocks. Bangladesh's currency, the taka, is expected to depreciate against the U.S. dollar from 2009 onward, though owing to rising foreign-exchange reserves in Bangladesh, the rate of depreciation is expected to be slower than it was in 2003–07 (EIU 2008). In the post-financial-crisis era, the taka has gained slightly against the U.S. dollar from the last quarter of 2008. Thus, in the post-financial-crisis era, Bangladesh is likely to suffer in level of exports and remittance inflows while gaining in import prices, though the expected exchange-rate depreciation might contribute to offsetting the threat, at least in part. As a consequence, Bangladesh may perform better than many other low-income countries in the face of the global economic slowdown.

Microfinance Sector Overview

Microfinance institutions (MFIs) emerged in Bangladesh starting in the early 1970s with the famous "Jobra" experiments of Dr. Muhammad Yunus and a number of other, government-led initiatives. These gave rise to the proliferation of numerous institutions that flourish in the country today. Bangladesh is generally considered to be a mature microfinance market, with a multitude of players and a sector that employs around 150,000 people (Credit and Development Forum 2006).

As noted earlier, 374 microfinance nongovernmental organizations (NGOs) were registered in Bangladesh as of December 2008, of 4,236 that had applied. The potential number that could qualify, given the major criteria of having 1,000 borrowers or Tk 4 million in principal loans outstanding, is 452. Thus, there are another 78 in the pipeline. The Credit and Development Forum (CDF) reported on 611 MFIs in a recent annual statistical compendium and stated in a discussion session in mid-2008 that it has 1,500 MFI linkage members that voluntarily report to it (CDF 2006).

The microfinance sector in Bangladesh comprises the following:

- Microfinance NGOs, with 11,715 branches serving about 24 million members and 19 million borrowers with total loans amounting to about $1,264 million and total savings/deposits of $410 million (Microfinance Regulatory Authority 2006);

- Specialized institutions, such as Grameen Bank;
- Wholesale lending institutions, of which the Palli Karma-Sahayak Foundation (PKSF) is dominant;
- Commercial banks (both private and state-owned), which provide $29,635 million in loans and with savings/deposit facilities of $35,647 million to the microfinance sector through 6,752 branches (Bangladesh Bank 2008); and
- Various administrative divisions of the government that offer microfinance lending schemes.

Microfinance NGOs are the most prolific of the organizations in the microfinance sector, accounting for almost 50 percent of the sector in terms of cumulative loans disbursed. The rest of the sector is dominated by Grameen Bank, accounting for almost 27 percent, and various banks—both state-owned and private—that account for almost 13 percent (CDF 2006). Figure 2.2 contains a breakdown of disbursements by category. Though the amount of loans made by microfinance institutions, by value, is less than that of commercial banks, it should be noted that microfinance institutions serve a large number of the poor people in the most remote areas of the country and therefore are at the forefront of the fight against poverty through provision of financial services to people who otherwise have no access to the formal banking system.

Figure 2.2   Cumulative Microfinance Loan Disbursements, December 2006

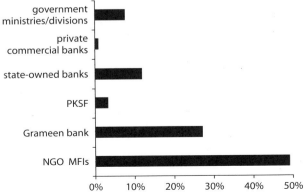

Source: CDF 2006.

The microfinance sector in Bangladesh is made up of four distinct classes of players: government entities, formal financial sector entities, private sector entities, and the MFIs themselves (figure 2.3).

Growth of the microfinance sector in Bangladesh can be attributed in large part to the creation of MFIs that have effective lending and operational models; the willingness of clients to take microcredit loans; the willingness of the government to provide wholesale financing via PKSF; and high population density that, coupled with high incidence of low-income people, provides an ample client base for the MFIs.

Microfinance Industry Regulators

Commercial banks in Bangladesh are regulated and supervised by Bangladesh Bank, while the credit organizations did not have a regulator for a long time. They were registered under the Societies Act as NGOs, but were not regulated. In 2006, the government decided to begin to regulate and supervise credit organizations through the Microcredit Regulatory Authority (MRA). The next section shows the efforts that the government has put into this activity thus far.

Microcredit Regulatory Authority

With the overarching objective of regulating the microfinance sector, the government of Bangladesh passed the Microcredit Regulatory Authority

Figure 2.3   Bangladesh Microfinance Players

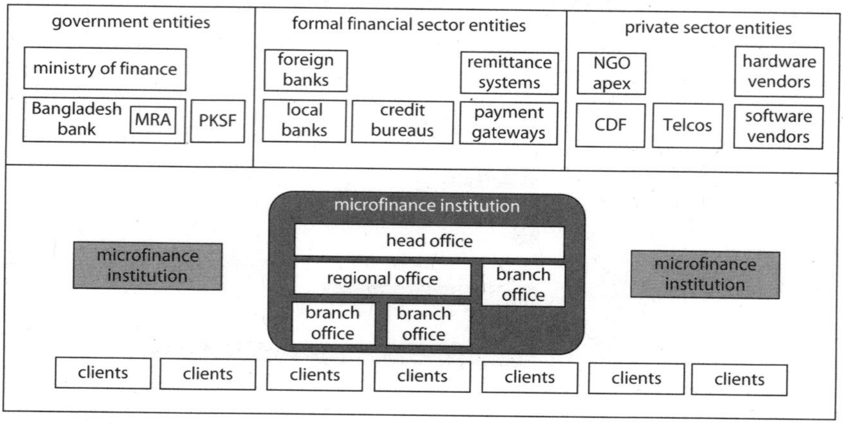

Source: Authors.

Act on July 16, 2006. This paved the way for the creation of the MRA under the aegis of the Bangladesh Bank.

The act governs the functions and authority of the MRA and provides prudential regulations for all MFIs in the country. Under the stipulations of the act, no MFI can carry out microcredit/microfinance activities in the country without a license from the MRA. MFIs must also report to the MRA according to specific guidelines and within time frames provided by the MRA.

Although still in its inception stage, the MRA has begun to develop the institutional and human capacity it needs to carry out its tasks. It has started the process of appearing "autonomous" by detaching itself from the Bangladesh Bank, building and moving into an office in a separate location, and has been engaging in dialogue with the broader MFI community. The MRA's organizational chart was approved in July 2008, and the manpower recruitment process began in August 2008.

The MRA has already solicited views on a number of issues, including the Microcredit Regulatory Authority Act, a possible prudential regulatory structure, and ways the MRA could be more effective. As the first steps in its journey, the MRA has begun the process of registering MFIs, and thus far has issued licenses to a total of 374 institutions. It has also shared its draft prudential regulations with the network of MFIs in the country and engaged in dialogue with stakeholders in an effort to make the regulations acceptable to all.

Bangladesh Bank

The Bangladesh Bank, the central bank, was established under the Bangladesh Bank Order of 1972 with retroactive effect to December 16, 1971. The general superintendence and direction of affairs and business of the bank are entrusted to a nine-member board. The governor of the Bangladesh Bank, who is appointed by the government of Bangladesh, acts as the chief executive officer and directs and controls all affairs of the bank on behalf of the board. The Bangladesh Bank provides oversight and prudential regulations for the formal financial sector and recently expanded its reach to the microfinance sector through the MRA.

Apex Funding Institution

Apex funding institutions have been set up by both governments and donors to provide funding and capacity-building support in countries that have a nascent microfinance sector with strong growth potential.

Palli Karma-Sahayak Foundation (PKSF) is one of those that were set up in the 1990s. These interventions were in response to lack of funding from commercial sources, including capital markets and other funding agencies, that are common today. The section below describes PKSF's role in the development of the microfinance sector in Bangladesh.

Palli Karma-Sahayak Foundation (PKSF)

The Palli Karma-Sahayak Foundation (translated—the Rural Employment Support Foundation), since its establishment in May 1990 by the government, functions as an apex microcredit funding and capacity-development institution in Bangladesh.

PKSF's three basic strategies are as follows:

- *It does not directly lend money to the clients.* Rather, it reaches the population through its partner organizations.
- *It has a focus on institutional development*, especially in developing the capacities of its partner organizations.
- *It acts as an advocate* for policies and regulations useful for supporting and strengthening the microcredit sector.

Though created by the government, legally, PKSF is a "company limited by guarantee" with a "not-for-profit company" status and is registered under the Companies Act of 1913/1994 with the Registrar of Joint Stock Companies (PKSF 2008).

As of 2008, PKSF had 196 partner organizations (MFIs that are debt funded by PKSF), reaching nearly 8 million borrowers. By 2006, PKSF had disbursed nearly $100 million to its partners (PKSF 2006). PKSF has four departments: (1) OOSA Department (small MFI partners), (2) BIPOOL Department (large MFI partners), (3) Administration Department, and (4) Audit Department. The total staff count stood at 237 as of December 2006 (PKSF 2006).

PKSF is an influential stakeholder in the microfinance sector and dominates the wholesale microfinance funding market. Though a large number of medium- and small-sized MFIs are waiting to access PKSF's low-cost funds, most are either rejected or are put through rigorous requirements before their applications for funding are accepted.

PKSF receives most of its microfinance wholesale funds from the government and multilateral and bilateral development partners—including the World Bank and Asian Development Bank. Microcredit allocations made by the government in its annual development budget are usually channeled to PKSF for on-lending to MFI partner organizations and to the broader MFI market. Special government allocations such as postdisaster recovery funds are also channeled through PKSF, as are World Bank funds, such as the $15 million loan for urban microcredit services made in May 2007 (MicroCapital 2007).

PKSF provides loans to small MFIs at rates ranging between 1 percent and 5 percent per year and to larger ones at 7 percent per year (PKSF 2006). The typical rate on commercial borrowing in Bangladesh, by comparison, is between 10 and 15 percent per year. In spite of this difference, some of the large- and medium-sized MFIs have already accessed commercial sources of funds to fuel their operations. Looking at the entire microfinance sector in 2006, PKSF funded only 14 percent of the microfinance NGOs' revolving loan funding needs, while commercial banks covered 18 percent (CDF 2006).

Although PKSF has counted several of the larger MFIs (such as ASA, BRAC, and PROSHIKA) as its partners since inception, the amounts lent to them have steadily decreased to an extent that a negligible amount of loans are outstanding to them—BRAC and ASA each had around 4 percent of their portfolio funded by PKSF in 2006 (ASA 2006; BRAC 2006). Recently, however, there has been a move by BRAC to borrow fresh funds from PKSF.

PKSF's role under the World Bank–financed Poverty Alleviation Microfinance Project. PKSF is a well-respected and established force within Bangladesh's financial sector. In 2001, the World Bank financed a $105 million Poverty Alleviation Microfinance Project to the government of Bangladesh with the objective of reducing poverty through expanding access to financial services to the poor through microfinance programs. A principal component of the project was capacity building to enhance the institutional and financial sustainability of PKSF and its partner organizations and to enhance PKSF's ability to disseminate best practices to increase the cost effectiveness of microfinance delivery throughout the country. The project's implementation completion report evaluated the outcome as satisfactory, with likely long-term and sustainable benefits. Borrower satisfaction and PKSF's performance as the lead implementation agency were deemed "highly satisfactory." Under the project, PKSF expanded its borrowing client base by 2.1 million—of which 90 percent were women. This level of outreach was 75 percent more than the appraisal target of 1.2 million. PKSF expanded its cumulative disbursements from Tk 1,100 million to Tk 7,900 million, while loans outstanding rose from Tk 732 million to

Tk 5,848 million. As a financer of small- and medium-sized partner organizations, PKSF's role was deemed "exemplary." According to the implementation completion report, PKSF "has firmly established itself as a leading and successful apex organization to extend funding to microfinance institutions of all sizes" (World Bank 2009). Because of the high standards of portfolio performance, reporting, staffing, and training that partner organizations needed to maintain in order to continue support from PKSF, PKSF is attributed with having led the sustainable development of the microfinance sector in Bangladesh.

Microfinance Market Size and Major Players

Academics and microfinance researchers in the Bangladesh have grouped microfinance NGOs in the country into five tiers, based on number of active borrowers: very large (more than 500,000 active borrowers), large (between 100,000 and 500,000 active borrowers), medium (25,000 to 100,000 active borrowers), small (5,000 to 25,000 active borrowers), and very small (fewer than 5,000 active borrowers).

While the microfinance market in Bangladesh hosts MFIs in all categories, it can be generally broken down into a few very large MFIs, some large MFIs, a handful of medium-sized MFIs, and nearly 1,000 MFIs with a narrow regional focus and borrowers numbering less than 25,000. Although mergers and acquisitions (of institutions or portfolios) have been predicted for some time given the maturity of the market, they are generally yet to happen.

Sectorwide reporting in microfinance is done on a voluntary basis to two major sources. In-country, annual reports are sent to CDF; globally, reports are sent to MIX (Microfinance Information Exchange) Market at frequencies determined by the MFIs (some do semiannual reporting, while others do annual reporting). The level of information disclosed to either is determined by the MFIs and neither CDF nor MIX perform audits to verify the accuracy of the information provided.

Looking at the 68 MFIs reporting from Bangladesh to MIX (figure 2.4), the following picture emerges: five very large MFIs cater to 86 percent of the active borrower population, 32 medium-sized and large MFIs serve 12 percent of total active borrowers, and the remaining 2 percent of the market of active borrowers is distributed among 31 small and very small institutions.

According to CDF statistics, of the 611 MFIs under its purview, only 14 have more than 100,000 active members, while some 218 MFIs

Figure 2.4   Active Borrowers by MFI Class

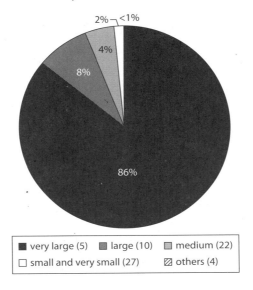

Legend	
■ very large (5)	■ large (10)	■ medium (22)
□ small and very small (27)	▨ others (4)

Source: MIX Market.

(about 36 percent of the total sample size) have fewer than 500 active members each.

The small loans are still heavily focused on female borrowers, who account for 89 percent of MFI clients. Though male clients increasingly are becoming MFI clients, they are served mostly in the microenterprise and small and medium enterprise (SME) loan segments. Of the 611 MFIs, almost 80 percent started operations after 1995 and have therefore been in business for around 10 years at most. Nearly 25 percent have no branch offices (they function only out of a head office), and only 3 percent have more than 50 branches in operation.

Information about the 68 Bangladeshi MFIs reporting to MIX Market is presented in table 2.1.[2] As can be seen, the microfinance market in Bangladesh, both in terms of size of loan portfolio and number of active borrowers, is dominated by very large institutions.

Grameen Bank
Grameen Bank was established in 1976 and transformed into a formal bank in 1983 under a special law passed by the Chief Martial Law Administrator at the time. The creation of Grameen Bank came about

Table 2.1   Bangladesh Microfinance Institutions: Loan Portfolio and Borrowers

	Name	Gross loan portfolio	Share of domestic micro-finance market	Number of active borrowers	Share of domestic micro-finance market
Very large:	Grameen Bank	$532,010,669	31.12%	6,707,000	28.28%
> 500,000 clients	BRAC	$528,787,592	30.93%	6,397,635	26.97%
(86% of borrowers)	ASA	$305,268,840	17.86%	5,163,279	21.77%
	PROSHIKA	$54,319,532	3.18%	1,587,166	6.69%
	TMSS	$38,555,615	2.26%	513,055	2.16%
Large:	BURO Bangladesh	$28,460,360	1.66%	354,020	1.49%
> 100,000 and	JCF	$22,914,310	1.34%	274,899	1.16%
> 500,000 clients	RDRS	$11,440,228	0.67%	257,292	1.08%
(8.14% of borrowers)	SSS	$25,174,774	1.47%	250,992	1.06%
	PMUK	$8,729,074	0.51%	171,021	0.72%
	Shakti	$16,610,216	0.97%	145,888	0.62%
	RRF	$11,511,553	0.67%	138,547	0.58%
	UDDIPAN	$11,229,824	0.66%	128,081	0.54%
	POPI	$5,364,837	0.31%	105,689	0.45%
	BEES	$7,573,579	0.44%	103,836	0.44%
Medium:	ESDO	$5,361,095	0.31%	96,088	0.41%
> 25,000 and	CODEC	$3,603,891	0.21%	80,682	0.34%
< 100,000 clients	DSK	$7,321,387	0.43%	80,005	0.34%
(4.42% of borrowers)	SKS Bangladesh	$3,465,288	0.20%	63,432	0.27%
	IDF	$5,389,021	0.32%	63,127	0.27%
	HEED	$5,015,412	0.29%	60,909	0.26%
	ASOD	$3,170,309	0.19%	60,419	0.25%
	COAST Trust	$3,555,768	0.21%	55,112	0.23%
	Wave	$3,363,492	0.20%	52,965	0.22%
	Sajida	$5,459,415	0.32%	50,927	0.21%
	PPSS	$2,856,767	0.17%	38,375	0.16%
	CCDA	$3,101,211	0.18%	37,240	0.16%
	PMK	$3,886,704	0.23%	36,470	0.15%
	DIP	$2,173,005	0.13%	35,242	0.15%
	CSS	$1,627,287	0.10%	34,133	0.14%
	DESHA	$2,039,300	0.12%	33,650	0.14%
	RIC	$1,778,757	0.10%	31,563	0.13%
	SDC	$2,238,327	0.13%	31,027	0.13%
	PBK	$1,745,200	0.10%	30,090	0.13%
	ASKS	$2,038,552	0.12%	25,996	0.11%
	AF	$1,653,595	0.10%	25,839	0.11%
	VERC	$2,796,694	0.16%	25,763	0.11%
	Subtotal (top 37)	$1,681,591,480	98.37%	23,347,454	98.43%
	Total reporting (68 MFIs)	$1,709,570,960	100.00%	23,717,187	100.00%

Source: MIX Market.

due to the identified need for a specialized bank to provide collateral-free loans to the poor—as demonstrated by Dr. Yunus and his experiments in microcredit. At the time of its inception, Grameen Bank was majority owned by the clients of the bank (savings of the borrowers accounted for a 51 percent stake) and the government held a 49 percent stake. The government nominated the board and had an active say in the functioning of the bank. Over time, as the bank grew, the government's stake gradually diminished.

According to MIX Market, as of December 2007, Grameen Bank had a loan portfolio of $532 million, catering to 6.7 million active borrowers. The organization had 20,885 staff members in 2006 and was present in all 64 districts of Bangladesh (CDF 2006).

Bangladesh Rural Advancement Committee (BRAC)

BRAC was established in 1972 and started its microfinance activities in 1974. It takes a holistic approach to development, undertaking a host of development activities—health, education, human rights, and social services—in addition to providing microfinance services. BRAC has a number of successful commercial entities, including Aarong (an outlet for products created by rural artisans), BRAC Bank, BRAC University, BRACNet (an Internet service provider), Documenta Ltd. a (software development firm), and Delta BRAC Housing Ltd. (a provider of commercial housing finance) (BRAC 2006).

BRAC's 2006 annual report stated that its sources of funds were member savings (42 percent), retained earnings (26 percent), loans from commercial local banks (22 percent), grants from donors (6 percent), and PKSF (4 percent).

As of December 2007, BRAC had a loan portfolio of $529 million and 6.4 million active borrowers, according to MIX Market. In 2006, BRAC had a total of 42,693 staff members, of whom 24,457 were dedicated to microfinance operations (BRAC 2006). The staff worked out of 1,498 branches extended across the country.

ASA

ASA was established in 1978 and began to focus exclusively on microfinance in 1991 as the sole mechanism for assisting the poor of the country. ASA is famous for its self-reliance (it is no longer dependent on donor aid) and its cost-effective microfinance model.

In 2006, ASA had a total of 18,400 staff members working in 2,931 branches in all 64 districts of Bangladesh. Its major sources of funds for that year were retained earnings (56 percent), member savings and security funds (34 percent), and PKSF (4 percent) (ASA 2006). At the end of 2006, ASA had a loan portfolio of $305 million and catered to 5.1 million active borrowers, according to MIX Market.

PROSHIKA

Established in 1976, PROSHIKA is another of the leading microfinance NGOs in Bangladesh. PROSHIKA works with a broad range of programs in organization building, education, and training, leading to income and employment generation, health education, and health infrastructure building, as well as environmental protection and regeneration. These are supported by policy advocacy and research activities related to the poorest of the poor.

At the end of 2006, PROSHIKA reported that it was working in 49 districts catering to about 1.7 million clients and had a loan portfolio of about $54 million. It had a staff of 3,900 in its microfinance program (CDF 2006).

Thengamara Mohila Sabuj Shangha (TMSS)

TMSS was established as a Social Development Organization in 1980 and started its microfinance activities in 1987. As of mid-2007, TMSS had a total loan portfolio of $38 million and a total of 513,000 active clients (MIX Market). According to the reports directly from the organization, it worked in 43 districts of the country and employed almost 3,600 microfinance staff members.

Microfinance Networks

Microfinance networks were established to carry out advocacy roles for their members and to ensure that transparency and accountability becomes the basis of their members' operations. Many of these networks also provide capacity building and technical assistance support to their members. Some have been undertaking consultancy and research activities to augment the incomes from fees in order to enhance their sustainability. In Bangladesh, the networks described below provide service at two levels. The CDF serves the national Bangladesh stakeholders, while the International Network of Alternative Financial Institutions (INAFI) is a global network. The sections below show the operations of these two networks.

Credit and Development Forum (CDF)

In the early 1990s, a number of stakeholders within the microfinance NGO sector met to share lessons and ideas and determined that it would be beneficial to them all to have a professional networking platform. With help from PRIP Trust[3] and the Swiss Agency for Development and Cooperation (SDC), they formed the first MFI-centric professional network in Bangladesh, CDF, in 1992.

CDF is registered as a "not-for-profit company, limited by guarantees" (CDF 2006) and is funded by contributions from its members as well as donor funding. CDF defines its four core services as follows:

- *Capacity building.* These include training on a wide range of topics for CDF's member MFIs. CDF organized a total of five training courses in 2006.
- *Network, advocacy, and research.* These include organizing advocacy seminars and workshops, eight of which were conducted in 2006.
- *Microcredit linkage program (MLP).* This includes linking MFIs with commercial banks to build their business relationships. It also includes training MFIs on methods used to approach banks for accessing funds. In 2006, CDF reported having around 44 partner MFIs under its bank linkage program.
- *CDF-Concern partnership project.* With the help of the NGO Concern Worldwide, CDF assists its partner MFIs in accessing formal financial institutions such as banks and government development assistance resources (CDF 2006).

CDF is now the most prominent source of microfinance-sector information in Bangladesh. Beyond just covering the microfinance NGOs, CDF reports holistically on the sector, including activities of specialized public institutions; banks (including specialized ones such as Grameen Bank and Krishi Bank); and ministries and government divisions— sectors that other sources of information, such as MIX Market, fail to capture. CDF's flagship product is the annual "Microfinance Statistics," which reports on the microfinance sector in Bangladesh and is cited as an authoritative source of information.

As of 2006, CDF had 19 professional and seven support staff members. CDF's income and expenditures for that year are illustrated in table 2.2. Major donors to CDF are Concern Worldwide, SDC, and the Dutch NGO Cordaid. Main local sources of income for CDF include payments from

Table 2.2   CDF's 2006 Income and Expenditure

	Amount in takas	Amount in $
Income: donor contributions	1,308,296	19,240
Income: local sources	8,558,717	125,863
Expenditures	9,474,631	139,333

Source: CDF 2006.

network members, fees earned from local training, and income from sales of annual publications.[4]

International Network of Alternative Financial Institutions

The International Network of Alternative Financial Institutions (INAFI) is a global network of microfinance practitioners consisting of 118 NGOs and MFIs operating in 38 countries in three continents. It is headquartered in The Hague and registered under Dutch law. Its activities in Bangladesh encompass capacity building of microfinance NGOs, thematic conferences, seminars, credit rating. It also campaigns and lobbies with concerned stakeholders on specific issues.

INAFI membership within Bangladesh includes ASA, BRAC, BURO Bangladesh, IIRD, PBK, PROSHIKA, Shakti Foundation, TMSS, United Development Initiative for Programmed Action, BASA, People's Oriented Program Implementation, ASHRAI, PADAKHEP, South Asia Partnership Bangladesh, Sajida Foundation, Gana Unnayan Kendra (GUK), Society for Social Service (SSS), Samaj Kallyan Sangstha (SKS), Ghashful, Joypurhat Rural Development Movement (JRDM), Community Development Centre (CODEC), Snannyo Samaj Kallyan Sangostha (ASKS), and COAST Trust.

Formal Financial Sector

Several formal financial sector interventions are being used in the context of the microfinance sector. These interventions include: remittances, credit bureaus, and financial support that the commercial bank sector is beginning to provide to credit organizations, such as structured finance and other forms of credit facilities.

Commercial Banks

Some local and foreign commercial banks have begun actively lending to MFIs in Bangladesh and, as mentioned above, MFIs are borrowing from these sources despite the higher rates. Local banks, such as BRAC Bank and The City Bank, have been active in lending to MFIs in the country at commercial rates. Although the volume of loans currently provided by these banks is relatively low, positive experiences should lead to more banks joining in to increase the availability of funds to the MFIs.

Citibank NA and Standard Chartered are the most active in Bangladesh—both have committed, globally, to providing MFIs with funding. Both institutions have been cautiously evaluating the sector for some time and have dedicated institutional resources to microfinance. Additionally, both institutions have formed strategic partnerships with agencies such as the German development bank KfW, the International Finance Corporation (IFC), and the Dutch entrepreneurial development bank FMO in various countries around the world to provide financing to MFIs.

Citibank NA is the most prominent of the international commercial banks around the world that have partnered with MFIs. It provides direct and structured financing, access to local capital markets, leasing, individual lending through MFI partners, foreign exchange and interest rate hedging, remittances, and insurance (see Citigroup [2008] for more details).

Standard Chartered committed to establishing a $500 million microfinance facility, to be utilized over five years across Asia and Africa, at the Clinton Global Initiative in September 2006 (Standard Chartered 2008). The bank focuses on several key areas of microfinance, including channeling funds to the microfinance sector, partnering with development organizations to develop innovative ways to support the sector by better managing the risks, and providing technical assistance. Standard Chartered (2008) states that it has 41 MFI partners in 13 countries across Asia and Africa and a total microfinance portfolio of $170 million.

Some notable deals in the microfinance funding sector in Bangladesh include the following:

- July 2006: Citibank NA Bangladesh entered into a structured finance deal to securitize a portion of BRAC's loan portfolio, backed by KfW and FMO, for $180 million local currency equivalent over a period of six years.
- December 2007: A consortium led by Standard Chartered provided a $55 million loan to BRAC.
- February 2008: IFC teamed up with Citibank NA Bangladesh to loan $22 million to the microlending efforts of BRAC.

- March 2008: Citibank NA Bangladesh provided a total of $65 million local currency equivalent credit facility to BRAC, BURO, Shakti Foundation for Disadvantaged Women, and TMSS. The major purpose of this financing was to support the microcredit and small- and medium-enterprise financing in Bangladesh after floods and cyclones.
- June 2008: Citibank NA Bangladesh extended a $10 million credit facility to ASA.

Such moves indicate a clear willingness on the part of the larger MFIs to borrow from commercial sources. Mid-sized MFIs also continue to borrow from domestic commercial sources.

Providing microfinance services in some of the world's most densely populated, least-developed countries calls for a huge amount of financial resources—something that donor funding alone cannot fulfill. At the end of the day, therefore, MFIs must learn to sustainably borrow from commercial sources of funds to fuel their growth. This partnership between MFIs and commercial banks is key to ensuring access to financial services for the world's poor and underserved.

Remittances

Bangladesh is one of the world's major exporters of unskilled labor. Bangladeshi workers can be found all over South Asia, the Middle East, and Europe. Remittances by these workers have a major impact on the economy of the country—in fact, they are second to the ready-made garment industry as a source of foreign exchange earnings. According to estimates made by the Economist Intelligence Unit (2008), remittance inflows to Bangladesh stood at $4.2 billion in the first seven months of fiscal year 2007/08, nearly $1 billion higher than the first seven months of fiscal year 2006/07. According to data published by the Bangladesh Bank, remittances stood at $6 billion in fiscal year 2006/07. But as noted in chapter 1, remittance inflows are likely to decline in 2008 and 2009 due to the global financial crisis.

Formal remittances are made via bank transfers—where some state-owned banks and private commercial banks have specialized services—or via international money transfer agents such as Western Union. Bangladeshi commercial banks such as National Bank Limited and BRAC Bank have entered into partnership with Western Union to provide remittance services through their branches capitalizing on Western Union's global network.

Credit Bureaus

In 2004, PKSF attempted to create a credit bureau database for the microfinance sector with funding from the World Bank. A software application was created by a local vendor and a hardware platform was procured for this purpose. The system, however, failed because backward linkages with granular client data of the MFIs was not created—the basic problem was that the MFIs themselves were not automated and therefore could not provide individual client records electronically, which were required to create the database.

The Bangladesh Bank has maintained a Credit Information Bureau (CIB) since 1992. Forty-nine banks and 27 financial institutions supply data to it.[5] As of end-2003, the CIB had information on 620,000 entities—including borrowers (firms and individuals), owners, and guarantors—and provided almost $14 billion worth of credit information. The major aim of the CIB is to provide credit guarantees for commercial borrowers.

The Bangladesh Bank is also committed to upgrading and automating the CIB, with support from the U.K. Department for International Development (DFID) and IFC. The scope of the project is to equip the CIB with resources necessary to be consistent with international standards and meet the demands of the financial sector. The new CIB application system will streamline the collection of data from banks/financial institutions and consolidate the collected data into an expanded central database with tools that will allow greater throughput and expanded analytical capabilities. An international tendering process to select a vendor was initiated in March 2008. The vendor is at the final stages of gathering the requirements from the CIB team at Bangladesh Bank. The official handover of the complete solution is expected to occur at the end of October 2010.

Microfinance Products and Services

All MFIs in Bangladesh offer a similar range of services: small- and medium-sized loans, various types of savings products, and microinsurance products.

Loan Products

The most common type of loan disbursed by MFIs, the small loan, is quoted on the flat-interest-rate calculation method and varies between 10 and 15 percent during the tenure of the loan (CDF 2006). This translates to an effective interest rate of 22–30 percent using the declining method and factoring in other costs. Small loans are typically repaid weekly with a tenure varying between 40 and 45 installments. In their internal calculations, the MFIs factor in holidays and missed payments and estimate that 45 installments are usually paid in 52 weeks.[6]

MFI loan products are made flexible to cater to a number of socioeconomic segments—in terms of loan sizes, interest rates, and repayment periods. The most common loan products are small loans, loans given to the "hardcore poor" or destitute population, seasonal agriculture loans, small business loans, microenterprise loans, and loans tailored for various income generation schemes. MFI clients are more frequently women than men. A typical loan product spread (taken from ASA) is shown in table 2.3. As of 2006, the average per-borrower loan outstanding among microfinance NGOs in Bangladesh was Tk 4,546 ($67). The average loan outstanding per male borrower remains higher than the average per female borrower, by about 30 percent, and loans disbursed in urban areas are larger than those disbursed in rural areas, by about 25 percent (CDF 2006).

Savings Products

In addition to loan products, MFIs offer various savings products: forced savings (mandatory savings deposits paid with each loan installment), voluntary savings (savings in addition to the mandatory savings), security deposits (a percentage of loan disbursed), long-term deposits, and deposit pension schemes.

The MFIs pay interest on the average savings balance at various rates varying from 0 to 15 percent per year. The industry average is between 5 to 7 percent per year (CDF 2006).

For the microfinance industry in Bangladesh as a whole, female rural clients had net savings of around $276 million (rural women save the most of any demographic grouping) in 2006, and the industry had total savings of around $362 million. The net average savings balance of a member of a microfinance NGO was Tk 1,200 ($18) (CDF 2006).

Microinsurance

MFIs offer a wide range of microinsurance products. These range from keeping loan risk premiums to offering write-offs in the event of the borrower's death to medical and funeral arrangement costs in case of illness or death of either the borrower or someone in the borrower's immediate family. Premiums are either deducted from the member's account or

Table 2.3 Terms and Conditions of ASA's Loan Products

SI.	Description	Small (Female)	Small [Male]	Hardcore poor	Small business	SEL/IT/ Agri-business	BDS	Rehabilitation	Short term	Education
1	Group size	15–35	Individual	5–20	10–15	Individual	Individual	Individual	Individual	Group members children
2	Meeting provision	Weekly	No meeting	No meeting	Weekly/ monthly	No meeting	N/A	N/A	N/A	N/A
3	Service charge (flat rate)	12.5%	12.5%	12.5%	12.5%	12.5%	12.5%	Free	12.5%	10.0%
4	Realizable installment system for Tk 1,000 loan	Weekly Tk 25	Monthly Tk 94 (rest amount in 12th installment)	Weekly Tk 25/ monthly Tk 94 (rest amount in 12th Installment)	Weekly Tk 25/ monthly Tk 94 (rest amount in 12th installment)	Monthly Tk 94 (rest amount in 12th installment)	Weekly Tk 25/ monthly Tk 94 (rest amount In 12th installment)	Weekly Tk 25/ monthly Tk 94 (rest amount in 12th installment)	Weekly Tk 25/ monthly Tk 94 (rest amount in 12th installment)	Weekly Tk 22
5	Realizable number of weekly/monthly Installment	45	12	12	45/12	12/18/24	45/12	Flexible	Flexible	50
6	1st installment start from disbursement date	After 15 days	After one month	After one month	After 15 days/one month	After one month	After 15 days/one month	Flexible	Flexible	After 7 days
7	Loan risk premium	Tk 3/ thousand loan	Tk 5/ thousand loan	Tk 3/thousand loan	Tk 3/ thousand loan	Postdated check and promissory note on nonjudicial stamp	N/A	N/A	N/A	N/A

(continued)

Table 2.3 Terms and Conditions of ASA's Loan Products (Continued)

Sl.	Description	Small (Female)	Small [Male]	Hardcore poor	Small business	SEL/IT/ Agri-business	BDS	Rehabilitation	Short term	Education
8	Provision against risk premium, after client's death	Outstanding loan written off	Outstanding loan written off	Outstanding loan written off	Outstanding loan written off	N/A	N/A	N/A	N/A	NA
9	1st cycle loan	Tk 4,000–15,000	Tk 1000–4,000	Highest Tk 5,000	Tk 20,000–50,000	Tk 30,000–400,000	Highest Tk 5,000	N/A	Maximum Tk 100,000	Tk 3,000
10	Loan increase provision from 2nd to above cycles	Highest Tk 4,000	Tk 1,000	Highest Tk 2,000	Highest Tk 7,000	Depends on feasibility	N/A	N/A	N/A	N/A
11	Loan duration	One year	One year	Quarterly/ half-yearly/ yearly/ Flexible	One year	Highest 2 years	Flexible	N/A	1–3 months	One year
12	Cost of passbook, loan application, and appraisal fees	Free of cost	Free of cost	Free of cost	Free of cost	Appraisal fee (Tk 2 per 1,000)	Free of cost	Free of cost	Free of cost	Free of cost
13	Penalty for late payment	N/A	N/A	N/A	N/A	N/A	N/A	N/A	N/A	N/A

Source: Extracted from ASA's information brochure on June 2008.
Note: N/A = not applicable.

are contributed by the MFIs themselves. These microinsurance products are not passed on to secondary or formal insurance institutions, nor are they passed on to another agency in the manner common to the formal insurance industry.

Regulatory Regime

Microfinance NGOs in Bangladesh have long sought regulatory recognition as a specialized form of financial institution providing the working poor with collateral-free loans and taking their deposits for safekeeping. As such, MFIs have approached the government to provide legal definitions of MFIs so that they could be licensed (and thus regulated) and be allowed to form regulated microfinance banks.

With the emergence of numerous MFIs in Bangladesh and with the sector maturing to rival the formal financial sector—at least in terms of clients served—the government is also seeking mechanisms by which to formally regulate the sector. In 2006, with the passing of the Microcredit Regulatory Authority Act, the government recognized the need for the MFIs to be regulated and licensed but did not respond to their interest to register as microfinance banks with a less stringent regulatory regime. The current (2008) government's objectives with respect to regulation of the microfinance sector are twofold. The first is client protection, given a recent spate of fraud (misappropriation of members' savings) by several MFIs. The second objective is to provide increased structure to the industry to help it grow and access facilities typically reserved for formal financial institutions.

In 2008, the MRA circulated, on a restricted basis, draft microfinance regulations to CDF for discussion with its members. These regulations draw upon the Microcredit Regulatory Authority Act and encompass a number of issues beyond it.

Market Potential for Growth

On average, the loan portfolios of microfinance NGOs in Bangladesh grew by 28 percent in 2006 (CDF 2006). This was in keeping with industry average growth rates of around 20 to 23 percent in each of the past five years. Loan utilization by clients is distributed among the small business sector (43 percent), agricultural sector (27 percent), processing and industries sector (6 percent), transport sector (2 percent), social sector (2 percent), and miscellaneous (20 percent) (CDF 2006).

Bangladesh's moderate pace of economic growth, coupled with its high rate of population growth, leads the country toward high levels of unemployment, which ultimately leads to an increase in the number of people willing to engage in trade and/or business activities requiring the commitment of financial resources. With the proliferation of MFIs in the country and their willingness to provide increasingly large loans, MFIs are now catering to a previously unserved class of clients—those whose financial needs are too small for formal financial institutions but too large for traditional microfinance loans.

Based on anecdotal evidence and conversations with industry practitioners, demand for small-business loans is increasing. This can also be validated by looking at the amount of microenterprise loans disbursed by PKSF between 2002 and 2006 (PKSF 2006); see figure 2.5 for more details.

This rapid growth can be attributed to two major factors: (1) the "graduation" of clients from small loans to larger small-enterprise/business loans, and (2) lateral entry of new clients into the small-enterprise/business loan segment. It seems, however, that in most instances, the latter cases outweigh the former.

With larger loan sizes and an increasing focus on small-business clients, loan officers faced another set of challenges: how to evaluate existing

Figure 2.5   Growth in PKSF's Microenterprise Loan Portfolio

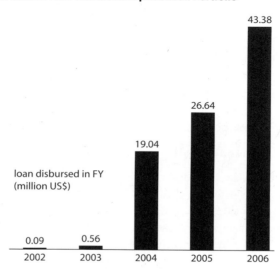

Source: PKSF's Annual Report, 2006.

businesses for their creditworthiness and how to assist clients in making their businesses succeed (thereby reducing portfolio risks). An emerging need for this segment of clients, and one that remains largely unmet, is to provide business development services to the microentrepreneurs. While some MFIs have in-house experts on subjects such as agriculture and livestock, clients' diverse range of business activities make it difficult for MFIs to have sector specialists for each individual line of business for which microenterprise loans are provided.

Market Outreach

In terms of geographical coverage, only 39 of the 611 MFIs under the watch of CDF have branch offices in more than five of Bangladesh's 64 administrative districts (CDF 2006). The 85 percent of MFIs covering five or fewer districts and with their specific regional focus should not be entirely discounted, however, as they play a vital role in providing localized services to grassroots communities and marginalized people who are unreachable by the larger MFIs.

Other Market Considerations

As stated earlier, microfinance sector reporting is done voluntarily by the MFIs to both CDF and to MIX. Although the number of MFIs that report to CDF is far higher than those that report to MIX, updating frequency seems to be higher in the latter.

For CDF, it usually takes the better part of a year to compile and analyze information provided by its partners and publish the results—sector information for 2006 was published in November 2007. This delay is because of a combination of factors, including delays in the MFIs providing information (often because, for accuracy, they wait to complete their financial auditing before sending information) and a lack of institutional information-processing capacity by CDF. Up-to-date information seems more likely to be available at MIX than at CDF. However, this information is limited to a small segment of the MFI population and does not cover government spending in the sector. In June 2008, only 68 MFIs reported to the MIX as opposed to 611 that reported to CDF in 2006.

Quality of data remains the major challenge for both CDF and MIX, since neither entity audits its partners to verify accuracy of the information. Large MFIs prefer to send audited annual reports to CDF, a trend that contributes to the time lag in the production of the reports by CDF.

Data provided to MIX, typically in an electronic format, are easier to send and are usually "cleaned up" to look attractive to potential donors and international financiers.

Traditionally, MFIs are very sensitive when it comes to sharing information or fully disclosing their financial information or performance. They tend to produce summary reports to report on their performance, which often leaves scope for data manipulation to make certain performance indicators and ratios look better. A case in point for this is the reporting of portfolio aging, a key indicator of an MFI's health. Most MFIs calculate this twice a year and rarely disclose the related findings on an ongoing basis.

One of the major stumbling blocks the creation of a centralized microfinance information reporting platform for Bangladesh must overcome is the reluctance for MFIs to share and disclose their information. The following section enumerates some of the market challenges that MFIs face in Bangladesh. Chapter 3 delves further into these challenges and describes how a shared ICT platform could ameliorate some of them.

Market Challenges

Lack of Common Reporting Methodology
MFIs do not follow a standard methodology for record keeping and information disclosure, leaving scope for data manipulation. The government of Bangladesh is seeking to standardize this through prudential regulations promulgated by the Microcredit Regulatory Authority (MRA).

Lack of Sector Reporting
Holistic information on the number of clients, client performance, client overlaps, and portfolio quality within the microfinance industry are all lacking. This not only affects the quality of government policy and financial interventions made but also limits foreign investor interest in the sector. Lack of holistic information is also one of the major issues facing the industry. Coupled with infrequent reporting to sources such as CDF and MIX Market, lack of holistic information makes the microfinance sector less than transparent in terms of monitoring its financial health.

Lack of Efficiency in MFIs
The MFI sector is paperwork intensive, and a large part of loan officers' staff time is spent doing record keeping and reporting tasks. Streamlining these processes will lead to operational efficiency gains and reduction of operational costs.

Substandard Data Quality

Most MFIs, large as well as small, maintain manual transaction records in ledgers and account books. These are filled in by loan officers day in and day out, often for hours on end. It is of little surprise, therefore, that data errors occur in these books. Oftentimes, these errors become apparent only when an automation project is under way and data cleanup needs to be carried out.

Client Overlap

Practitioners agree that client overlap (a single client taking loans from multiple MFIs) is widespread in the country. Anecdotal evidence collected from informal interviews by researchers indicates that the overlap could be as high as 20 to 30 percent. In certain areas of Bangladesh, field staff claim that overlap is as high as 50 percent. While the MFIs do not consider this to be a major issue, it needs to be monitored and researched for its impact on the industry—both on profitability and on delinquency. The current financial crisis offers important lessons that need to be taken into account.

Lack of Access to Capital for Growth

Most MFIs would like to have access to more funding to power their scale-up activities. They therefore would like to borrow from domestic and/or foreign commercial sources, a task that requires full and transparent record keeping and disclosure according to internationally-accepted principles.

Notes

1. Data in this section are taken from EIU (2008) and World Bank (2007).
2. The data in the table may not be the latest according to the institutions, but are is the latest aggregated data for those institutions that report to MIX Market. One major constraint is that data are not uniformly reported and take a long time to be analyzed, making obtaining a very current snapshot of MFIs (microfinance institutions) in Bangladesh almost impossible.
3. PRIP Trust is an NGO in Bangladesh whose major focus is to build institutional capacities of other NGOs and Civil Society Organizations.
4. All financial figures, sources of income, and staff counts were extracted from CDF (2006).
5. Information from presentation made by Bangladesh Bank GM on CIB: http://www.microfinancegateway.org/p/site/m/template.rc/1.9.25224 retrieved on December 3, 2009.
6. Based on industry consultation and discussions with MFIs.

CHAPTER 3

The Proposed Centralized ICT Platform

This chapter builds upon market research that was conducted in Bangladesh for this book and provides a conceptual framework for the role that information and communication technology (ICT) can play in addressing the significant market challenges that are currently constraining the transformation and modernization of the microfinance industry in Bangladesh. Technology can help microfinance institutions (MFIs) become more efficient and be more connected with field offices and customers. It can also allow the microfinance industry to offer a fuller suite of financial services, reduce overlap, improve outreach and impact, and become more integrated with the formal financial sector. The concept of a centralized ICT platform is introduced as an infrastructure that can link MFIs to each other, the government, the private sector, their networks, and the formal financial sector.

The Role of ICT in Meeting Bangladesh's Microfinance Market Challenges

The 1970s saw Bangladesh lead a revolution in banking for the poor by formalizing the concept of microfinance. Muhammad Yunus' now-famous Jobra social experiments allowed banking to no longer be limited to the privileged and the rich. Microfinance allowed the poor, for the first time in many countries, to access capital to use as credit in starting a new business, grow an existing business, emerge from an unforeseen crisis, and achieve growth and prosperity not envisaged prior to the advent of microfinance. Microfinance also helped empower women in societies where the role of women was often marginalized. Today, Bangladesh is home to some of the most reputable MFIs in the world. Innovations and best practices in microfinance that have emerged from Bangladesh are being used by countries in Africa, Latin America, the Middle East, and Asia, and MFIs in Bangladesh provide technical assistance to MFIs around the world.

Despite the tremendous success of the microfinance approach, MFIs in Bangladesh are looking for ways to do more. They would like to grow beyond their organic rates of growth in order to serve a greater number of poor people, not only in their home territory but also in developing countries in South Asia and around the world. They want to further their outreach into remote and rural areas and engage people who have thus far not enjoyed the benefits of microfinance. They wish to introduce new products and services so that microfinance can provide not only microcredit but a whole suite of financial services for the poor. They have identified new and appropriate sources of capital so they can further reduce interest rates for their clients and enjoy better financial well-being for their institutions. They are in the process of making their operations more efficient so they can save money, better serve their clients, and fully realize the difficult but necessary double bottom line: achieving financial sustainability *and* their declared social mission.

Bangladesh is in a position today to champion another revolution in the microfinance industry, a revolution that necessitates the use of technology and innovation. Such a revolution would push the microfinance industry into the next generation. Just as the country broke away from the tradition that banking is only for privileged and rich people, it can once again break away from the tradition that technology and innovation is only for sophisticated and rich industries.

Microfinance is a major industry in Bangladesh that currently serves 24 million borrowers. With technology and innovation, however, MFIs in Bangladesh could serve more people who do not have access to finance using branchless banking. They could improve access to financial services with the help of mobile banking and automated teller machines, innovations that can be rolled out even in rural areas. They could expand their product and service offerings to include savings, insurance, money transfers, and remittances. In addition, MFIs could make their day-to-day operations more efficient by allowing institutional headquarters to have up-to-date information about work being done in branch offices and with loan officers spread throughout the country. MFIs can do so at a lower cost without fully overhauling their operations and thus save money to help their financial bottom line.

As MFIs in Bangladesh provide a fuller suite of financial products and services, they assume a greater responsibility to ensure that savings deposits taken from the poor or hard-earned money channeled as remittances are in fact safe. In addition, the government assumes a greater responsibility to ensure that MFIs taking savings or remittances from the poor are in fact financially healthy and do not face the risk of becoming insolvent. A larger suite of financial products means greater responsibility and hence greater effort on the part of the whole microfinance industry to see that the poor are not exploited.

The use of technology in microfinance has not always been popular and has at times had limited success. MFIs in Bangladesh often see technology as a major expense and have difficulty justifying its use when their core business is so highly cost sensitive. Even when MFIs in Bangladesh decide to invest in technology, they still lack the skills to use technology or to fully mainstream technology down to their branch offices and to their loan officers. Because of cost and capacity issues, investment in technology often goes only halfway and not surprisingly produces half-formed results. Since only a handful of MFIs in Bangladesh even attempt to use technology, the microfinance industry as a whole does not benefit from technology-driven practices that should be common to the entire industry, such as the use of credit bureaus for screening out bad debtors. Innovations such as mobile banking are left to only a very few financial institutions that have the means to offer banking services over mobile phones or telecom service providers that can rely upon their own mobile subscriber base and not the entire microfinance delivery channel to offer mobile banking services.

Bangladesh has the potential, however, to broker another revolution in the microfinance industry, one that involves using a central microfinance technology platform. This new paradigm would make technology available to MFIs within Bangladesh in an affordable way so they can expand and innovate their operations and serve the poor in new, unprecedented ways. The paradigm rests on the fact that Bangladesh is a pioneer in the microfinance industry and that Bangladesh hosts one of the more widespread mobile and telecommunications networks among developing countries. Bangladesh is capable of embracing and adopting the paradigm and serving as an example to other countries that strive to use microfinance as a way to serve the poor.

Microfinance Technology: The Traditional Way

Though microfinance is a growing industry in Bangladesh, it is not without its challenges. Underlying these challenges is the need for MFIs in Bangladesh to be better equipped to serve a larger number of clients, with newer products and services, using a variety of delivery channels. Technology should allow MFIs to extend their outreach beyond their national borders. Today, however, technology goes only partway in helping MFIs improve their operations and does not bring about information advantages for the overall industry such as better reporting and reduced overlap.

Large MFIs in Bangladesh have already invested in technology for their operations. Some microfinance institutions are even developing customized software to map the processes of their individual institutions. The software is intended to reduce the workload of field staff and cater to the increasing number and complexity of products that the institutions are beginning to offer. Other large MFIs have purchased off-the-shelf software and streamlined the software into their operational processes. The large MFIs have thus been able to introduce computers in their head office and in branch offices, allowing them to automate their work, and are looking for ways to automate more.

Many small microfinance institutions in Bangladesh are just beginning to adopt information technology. They are charting out plans to buy computers, deciding between build-versus-buy decisions regarding software, and tapping into the growing automated teller machine (ATM) network to provide microfinance services to clients. However, plans are still being worked out and cost remains a major decision factor for such institutions. MFIs, however, unanimously underscore the importance of using information technology in their work.

The use of technology in microfinance in Bangladesh has effects at two levels: at the microfinance institutional level, and at the microfinance industry level. Figure 3.1 illustrates these effects.

Within Microfinance Institutions

At the microfinance institutional level, as noted, the use of technology is limited, as most MFI operations are currently processed either on paper, with limited management-information systems, or with the exchange of Excel spreadsheets over e-mail. Loan officers collect transactional information from clients mostly in paper form and report to the branch offices. Branch offices summarize transactional information collected

Figure 3.1   Technology Use within MFIs and the Microfinance Industry

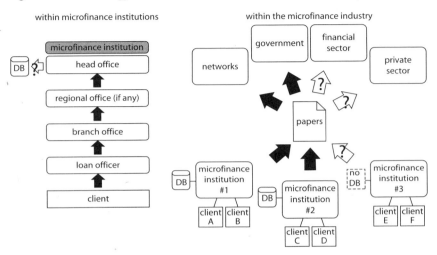

Source: Authors.
Note: DB = electronic database. The diagram illustrates a simplified view of technology in microfinance. In reality, an MFI may have electronic databases in branch offices, regional offices, and the head office.

from all loan officers and send it to the head office either directly or via a regional office. The information flow from the branch office to the head office is done manually or partially electronically on a weekly or monthly basis. The head office accumulates all information from all branch offices and stores it in an electronic database, a paper register, or both. The head office manages its entire operational structure based on this information exchange and faces a challenge when it does not have up-to-date information about work being done at the branch office or loan-officer level.

Within the Microfinance Industry

At the microfinance industry level, information is fragmented, and the limited and inconsistent use of technology precludes potential collective benefits for the overall industry. Some MFIs report a summary of client and portfolio information on a voluntary basis in response to paper surveys, while others do not. Information collected and summarized from paper surveys is available in paper form for review by the government and other industry stakeholders. No two MFIs exchange information about their clients with one another and are thus not able to differentiate between good and bad new customers.

Challenges

A number of challenges are apparent in the microfinance industry's operations in Bangladesh.

Information is paper-centric and not always timely. At the microfinance industry level, information is exchanged among various stakeholders in paper form and information handling is done manually. Industry reports are produced at best on a yearly basis. It is difficult to establish how the microfinance industry is performing on a given day, week, or month based on how information is collected presently.

Information is not complete. MFIs share information about their loan portfolios and clients on a voluntary basis only. Because such information is obtained from some MFIs and not from others, it is not possible to get a complete snapshot of the entire microfinance industry of Bangladesh.

Information is not verifiable. There are currently no systematic ways to verify the information provided by the MFIs. Though some mechanisms have been put in place by government authorities to audit the financials prepared by MFIs, such efforts are thus far limited. There is a need to assess the quality of information collected as MFIs expand into providing savings and remittance services to people in Bangladesh.

Head offices need more information about work being done in branch offices and by loan officers. MFI head offices do not have a single online window to show how business is going on in a branch office or with a loan officer at any instant of time. Information is exchanged between loan officers, branch offices, and the head office using paper, often manually. The information exchange process brings into question the timeliness and accuracy of information.

Microfinance institutions do not share information with one another. Each MFI uses its own local database or paper register to record what microcredit was given and to which client. No two MFIs share information about their clients. As indicated in figure 3.1, MFI 1 serves clients A and B, and MFI 2 serves clients C and D. MFI 1 knows everything about clients A and B but nothing about clients C and D. If client C defaults on MFI 2 and wishes to secure a new microloan from MFI 1, the latter has no way of knowing that client C is not a good client. There is no industry-wide credit bureau to help MFIs 1 and 2 to evaluate and maintain a credit profile of each customer. MFIs in Bangladesh may be able to overcome the risk of overlap by building trust with their clients and using field staff that have knowledge about the local markets. But such an approach runs the risk of not being sustainable, especially as MFIs scale up their operations. The challenge becomes a lot more difficult as MFIs begin to serve areas outside Bangladesh. Relying upon customer loyalty as a way to mitigate the risk of overlap requires a highly managed corporate environment that stresses the operational ability of the institution in question. As the number of clients increase substantially, a lot more information is needed to build, maintain, and monitor customer loyalty. Similarly, relying upon the knowledge of field staff runs the risk of knowledge loss because of employee turnover. As MFIs expand and begin to offer more complex products, they will need to have high-quality information about their clients and their operations in order to stay effective.

Microfinance institutions require capital and capacity to use technology. Technology is an expensive endeavor and MFIs face capital constraints in any effort to fully use technology. Even when MFIs are able to invest in technology, they do not always have the skills to use it properly. They thus require relief in the form of a low-cost technology solution that can lower their capital constraints and an outsourced technology solution that can reduce their capacity constraints.

Scaling up will be a challenge in the future. Because MFIs rely on paper-based transactional and informational flow, they may face challenges down the road as they try to scale up their operations. Use of a paper-based approach can overload operations if an MFI were to exponentially increase its customer base in a short amount of time.

New products and services can be difficult to launch. Because most transactional work is currently not done electronically and information is not recorded in an electronic database, new products and services such as mobile banking may be difficult to bring about for many MFIs.

Remittance flows can be limited. Because most microfinance transactional work is not done electronically and information is not recorded in an electronic database, remittances to or from Bangladesh via the microfinance delivery channel may be difficult to bring about.

The formal financial sector is not a full participant. The financial sector is currently not a major participant in the microfinance industry of Bangladesh. Commercial banks do not have adequate information about the financial health of MFIs or the credit profile of the customers these institutions serve. As a result, MFIs are not able to raise capital from commercial banks, and commercial banks are not able to provide financial services to the poor through the microfinance delivery channel.

The private sector is not a full participant. Telecom service providers currently do not have access to the microfinance delivery channel to offer services such as mobile banking to the poor in Bangladesh. Likewise, MFIs are not able to employ the vast mobile subscriber base to expand their financial services outreach. Technology vendors from the private sector could better serve the microfinance industry by offering computer hardware, software, products, and utilities.

Policy making and regulation are a challenge. Since the information obtained about the state of the microfinance industry in Bangladesh is not complete and there is an absence of timely and high-quality information, it is difficult for the government to know how the industry is performing and to formulate timely policy and regulatory decisions.

Centralized ICT Platform: The New Paradigm

Technology can help revolutionize the microfinance industry of Bangladesh and overcome some of the above-mentioned challenges. Technology, however, must be introduced in a way that it can serve the majority of MFIs in Bangladesh in a simple, cost-effective, and scalable manner.

The new paradigm presented in this book posits that technology can be centralized for Bangladesh's microfinance industry and be deployed to individual institutions throughout Bangladesh. Because technology is centralized, it exploits economies of scale and offers a cost-effective solution for all MFIs. Because an ICT platform is run out of one center, the skills required for running the center are collected in one place and outsourced from individual MFIs. The outsourced approach alleviates capacity constraints on individual institutions. Because technology is designed to be flexible, individual MFIs retain their competitive edge and use technology on an as-needed basis to strengthen their core competencies.

The new paradigm based on a centralized ICT platform would help connect all microfinance industry stakeholders with one another. It would bring about an information flow that allows MFIs to learn from one another. It would enable microfinance industry networks to know about the workings of the industry at any given point in time. It would allow the financial and the private sectors to tap into the vast delivery channel offered by microfinance. And it would provide the government with timely information for use before deciding to intervene strategically at crucial moments to help overcome any key challenges faced by the microfinance industry.

Figure 3.2 illustrates the role of the centralized ICT platform. First, the platform helps the head office, regional office, branch office, and loan officers of a single MFI connect with one another. Second, it helps all the industry stakeholders within the microfinance sector in Bangladesh to connect with one another.

Elements of a Centralized ICT Platform

The centralized ICT platform would consist of the following main elements:

- *A common management information system.* This is a minimal set of core microfinance software that would allow each MFI to perform its daily operations. The common software would be customizable so that individual needs of different MFIs can be met. Each head office, regional office, branch office, and loan officer would have the capability to connect to the centralized ICT platform, access an individual account, and conduct daily operations.

- *A common database.* This is a database capable of holding all data needs of all MFIs in Bangladesh. Each institution's data would be guaranteed to be secure and not accessible by anyone but the institution owning the data.

- *Computers.* A data center would hold all computing equipment, including computer servers, backup facilities, power backup units, and support functions.

Benefits to Microfinance Institutions

At the microfinance institutional level, the centralized ICT platform would bring about several benefits:

- *Low-cost technology.* By exploiting economies of scale, the centralized ICT platform would offer a low-cost solution for all technology needs of MFIs.

Figure 3.2   Role of a Centralized ICT Platform

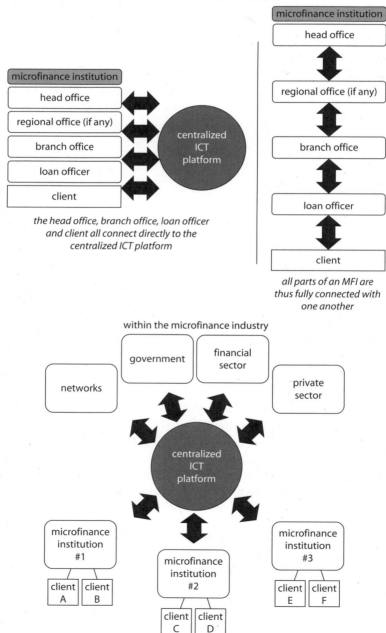

within microfinance institutions

the head office, branch office, loan officer
and client all connect directly to the
centralized ICT platform

all parts of an MFI are
thus fully connected with
one another

within the microfinance industry

Source: Authors.

- *Fewer technology-related skills required.* By bringing all outsourced technology needs of MFIs in one place, the centralized ICT platform would alleviate the capacity constraints faced by individual MFIs.

- *Head office connected to regional offices, branch offices, and loan officers.* Since the head office, regional offices, branch offices, and loan officers all connect to the same centralized ICT platform, the head office would have the capacity to know on a per-minute basis how business is going in any part of its institution.

- *Greater operational efficiency through the use of technology.* MFIs achieve greater efficiency in day-to-day operations by using technology. Information would no longer need to be collected in paper form or be transmitted via e-mail. Staff members would be able to focus their efforts on their core strengths, which are to provide financial services to the poor. The centralized ICT platform would handle all technology-related issues.

- *Ability to grow at a fast pace with the help of branchless banking.* MFIs would be able to use technology to grow at a faster pace, while achieving efficiency gains and lowering overall costs. Branchless banking is one way by which MFIs would be able to significantly expand outreach and serve rural and remote areas otherwise outside the purview of these institutions.

- *Ability to offer new products and services, including mobile banking and automated teller machines (ATMs).* MFIs are better positioned to introduce new products and services when information is collected and distributed electronically using the centralized ICT platform. The platform would also offer the provision to introduce new electronic applications such as mobile banking and automated teller machines that are currently nonexistent or not widespread in Bangladesh.

Benefits to the Microfinance Industry

The centralized ICT platform would also bring about important benefits at the microfinance industry level:

- *Increased information sharing and reduced overlap.* By providing a common database for all information, the centralized ICT platform would allow MFIs to share selected credit information about clients with one another. An industry-wide microfinance credit bureau would be created as an application within the centralized ICT platform. The government has issued national identity cards that would help in reducing overlap incidence.

- *Better access to capital.* The centralized ICT platform would also allow the MFIs to be connected with the formal financial sector. MFIs would thus be able to raise new capital directly from commercial banks and obtain more competitive interest rates.

- *Broader range of financial service offerings via payment systems.* MFIs would be able to use the centralized ICT platform to connect to the financial infrastructure of the financial sector, including payment systems, and thus be able to offer a fuller suite of financial services to the poor.

- *Ability to offer remittance services.* MFIs would be able to use the centralized ICT platform to connect to the financial infrastructure of the financial sector to provide remittance services to microfinance clients.

- *Ability to offer mobile banking.* MFIs would be able to use the centralized ICT platform to connect with telecom service providers and tap into the vast mobile subscriber base as a delivery channel for financial services.

- *Improved formal financial services to the poor.* Local and commercial banks would be able to connect with the MFIs through the centralized ICT platform and provide financial services to microfinance clients.

- *Better private-sector services to the poor.* Private-sector players such as telecom service providers would be able to connect with the MFIs through the centralized ICT platform and thus tap into the vast delivery channel of the MFIs to serve the poor.

- *Improved access to timely, accurate information.* MFIs would have access to more reliable and up-to-date information about the workings of the microfinance industry at any point in time.

- *Government ability to intervene if necessary.* With complete, accurate, and timely information about the entire microfinance industry, the government would be able to make better policy decisions and regulate at a lower cost. The government also would be in a position to intervene strategically to correct problems faced by the microfinance industry.

Outcomes of Centralized ICT Platform Implementation

A centralized ICT platform for the microfinance industry of Bangladesh would bring about the following outcomes:

- *A microfinance industry that serves more people with newer products and services.* Each MFI would be connected with its regional offices, branch offices, loan officers, and clients. Each MFI would be capable of providing additional products and services, such as mobile banking, branchless banking, and automated teller machines (ATMs), with the help of technology. And each MFI would be capable of serving more people even in remote, rural areas. See figure 3.3.

- *Reduced overlap.* MFIs would be able to share credit information about their clients with one another, as a centralized ICT platform would

Figure 3.3   Use of Technology by MFIs to Provide New Products

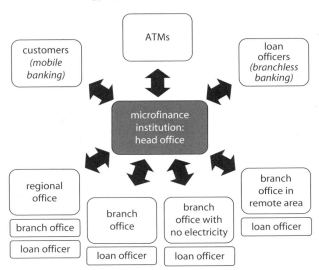

Source: Authors.

implement a credit bureau for microfinance clients as an application. See figure 3.4.

- *Government safety nets.* Government bodies would be able to channel payments through the centralized ICT platform and the microfinance network to beneficiaries throughout Bangladesh. See figure 3.5.

- *More accurate, online industry information.* Because information would be collected and distributed electronically, it would be more accurate and complete and available online. See figure 3.6.

- *A more integrated formal financial sector.* The microfinance industry would be integrated with the formal financial sector. The financial sector would reach out to the poor. The MFIs would connect with commercial banks and international financial institutions. See figure 3.7.

Figure 3.4   Technology Use to Overcome Overlap

Source: Authors.

Figure 3.5   Technology and Provision of Safety Nets

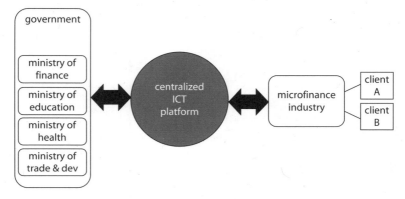

Source: Authors.

Figure 3.6   Technology and Provision of Accurate Online Data

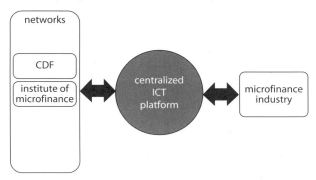

Source: Authors.

Figure 3.7   Integration of the Financial Sector

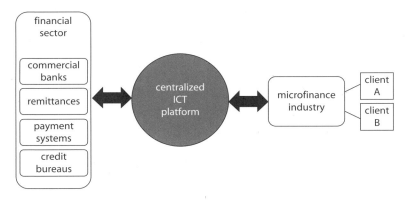

Source: Authors.

- *A more vibrant private sector.* The private sector would be more vibrant and a player in the microfinance industry. Telecom service providers would be able to reach the poor. Technology vendors would be able to serve the needs of the microfinance industry. See figure 3.8.

- *A more informed government.* With availability of good information, the government of Bangladesh would be able to make better policy decisions and make more effective regulations at a lower cost. See figure 3.9.

Figure 3.8   Centralized ICT Platform and the Private Sector

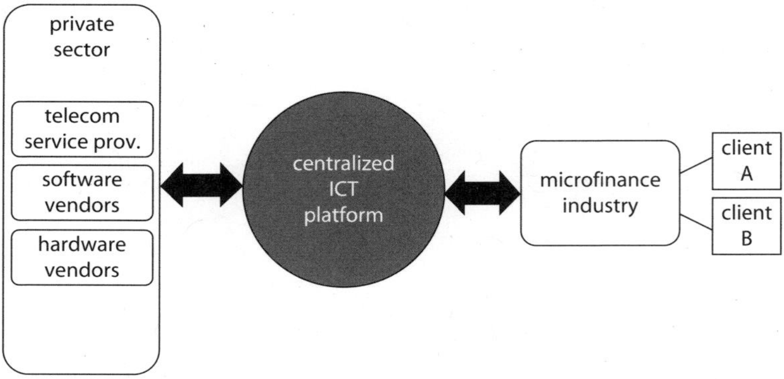

Source: Authors.

Figure 3.9   Provision of Accurate Information for Government Policy Making

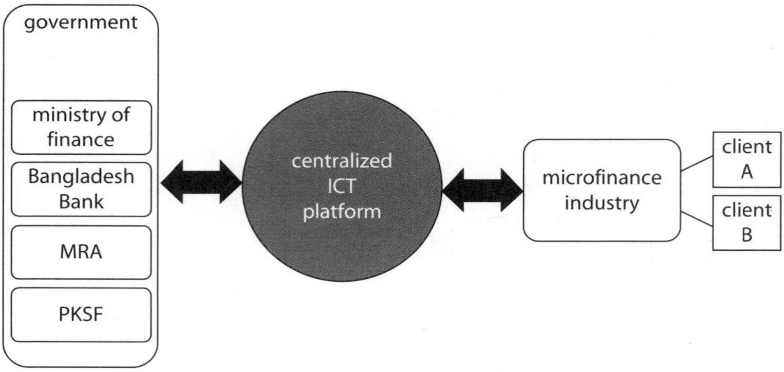

Source: Authors.

How to Develop a Centralized ICT Platform

Developing a centralized ICT platform for the entire microfinance industry of Bangladesh is a tall order. At minimum, there are three aspects of
the centralized ICT platform that require further examination: the
enabling environment, the technology design, and the institutional
design, as shown in figure 3.10.

Figure 3.10   Centralized ICT Platform Aspects

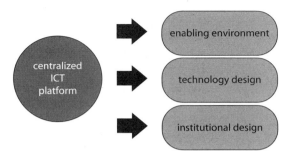

Source: Authors.

Each of these aspects and the emerging international practices related to them is discussed in greater detail in the remainder of this book. Practical insights into developing a centralized ICT platform for the microfinance industry of Bangladesh accompany the discussion.

CHAPTER 4

Emerging International Practices

Technology usage in microfinance is trending in new directions due to lower costs for connectivity and computing. The recognition of the need for a centralized microfinance platform has emerged, illustrated by efforts in a variety of countries by diverse actors. It is driven chiefly by the recognition that (1) microfinance providers, with only their own individual resources, will continue to make suboptimal technology choices, and (2) microfinance services, in order to expand to meet demand, must be capable of connecting to mobile-device-driven financial services. In this chapter, emerging best practices from a variety of efforts from around the world are examined as they pertain to a centralized microfinance platform.

New Innovations

A number of initiatives have begun to attempt to solve the problem of a lack of management information system (MIS) automation in microfinance, while taking advantage of trends in mobile connectivity. These trends include open source, financial switches, and hosted shared solutions.

Open-Source Models

Open-source models are aimed at creating collaborations on common functionality and creating virtuous cycles of software development. In microfinance, at least two efforts are under way. The first is Mifos, a project of the Grameen Foundation, aimed at Grameen-style operations and implemented in India and Kenya. The second is OFMS, implemented in a number of Central Asian countries. In Nepal, Magnus Consulting has started to implement Mifos with two microfinance institutions (MFIs).

On-Demand Software

On-demand software as a service model is one type of hosted solution, whereby a company creates a common platform and offers it for use by many users or companies. Salesforce.com, which was recognized for essentially creating this new business/technology model, has launched a Microfinance Edition as a shared platform. The platform is hosted in the United States and serves Fortune 1,000 companies around the world.

Financial Switches

Financial switches allow the microfinance industry to enable a better mix of products, reach more customer markets, and open new delivery channels. According to a leading expert on the subject (Reveille 2008), MFIs face two options in terms of financial switches. The first option is for MFIs to keep their own systems and develop ways of interfacing with payment-processing systems that are on the horizon. The second is for new application service provider (ASP)–hosted models to allow MFIs to share a common platform. The two options are shown in more detail in figure 4.1.

Figure 4.1   ASP-Hosted Models

option 1 – basic MFI joins payments network without new CBS

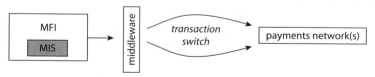

option 2 – MFI replaces/gets new CBS through ASP model (remote hosted, web-delivered)

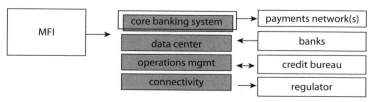

Source: Authors.

Hosted Models

In general, hosted models are either direct hosting service models or software as a service (SaaS) models, the latter of which are based on the ASP model and always includes a Web browser as the front end. Direct service models are essentially outsourcing the hosting and servicing of the software application and can involve one or more customers in a common configuration at a fixed location.

Software as a Service in ASP

Under an ASP model, a specific software package is offered online, thereby lowering the cost of technology acquisition for end users. These ASP models have been used in the finance, insurance, customer relationship management, inventory management, and other industries. This model, however, had challenges meeting expectations around flexibility and extensibility, particularly with existing client-server architectures, and gave way in 2000–01 to software as a service (SaaS), which follows the same precepts but is a native Web application, thereby reducing installation requirements at the client machine to only a Web browser. A number of new SaaS players in the financial services industry, led by Intaact and NetSuite, offer full accounting systems with integrated front-office functionality on demand. Another type of on-demand software, Google's desktop productivity suite of word processing and spreadsheets, is also spreading. And as a sign of the times, small-business software provider Quickbooks now has an SaaS offering. Open source, which now runs the majority of Web traffic, is a key component of the strategies of IBM, Sun, and other large technology companies and has led to the creation of new models that directly challenge the commercial off-the-shelf models.

Case Studies: Centralized Platforms for Microfinance

Among the greatest challenges that microfinance providers around the world face in implementing standards-compliant, high-quality back-office systems are (1) high up-front cost of the solution, (2) high requirements for connectivity, (3) the necessary level of sophistication of the technical team to support and maintain the systems, and (4) high ongoing costs. Many MFIs are now aware that one way to mitigate these challenges is to provide a generalized, high-quality MIS to a number of small financial institutions in one country through an outsourced or ASP or the more recent SaaS model. In such models, a vendor or vendors enter the market to provide a centralized solution that can be shared by a number of microfinance providers.

It is important to note that, because the introduction of centralized information communication technology platforms for microfinance delivery is still a relatively new innovation, the cases described below are in their start-up phases.

FINO: India

FINO (Financial Information Network & Operations Ltd) is a technology company that was incubated for two years within ICICI Bank in India, starting in 2004. At the time, ICICI Bank had an established practice of wholesale lending to more than 60 microfinance providers across the country and had plans to grow its portfolio to more than 200 MFIs. The key challenge was in obtaining high-quality and timely data from the microfinance partners to adequately monitor their loans.

According to FINO materials, the company is a multibank-promoted company that provides smart card–based multi-application solutions to the "bottom of the pyramid people." It is an ASP that assists the banking, microfinance, insurance, and government sectors in providing their services to the unbanked and unserved people of India. Following a model of financial inclusion, FINO strives to cover the very large number of people— 500 million—living in rural areas of India.

FINO's microfinance platform solution consists of a remote data-capture device combined with a back-office banking solution. The remote device was originally based on Simputer and had a proprietary, biometric application developed for FINO's needs, but over time the company migrated to a biometric, smart-card solution provided by BGS Smartcard Systems, a company based in Austria. The banking system selected was i-flex, a company based in India with a global banking customer base.

As of July 2006, FINO hoped to reach 200 microfinance providers by March 2007, with the ultimate goal of reaching 300 million to 400 million people with the solution (*The Hindu Business Line* 2006). A press release of April 2008 announced that the company had succeeded in enrolling 1 million financial clients on its platform (FINO 2008). While impressive, this number is only a small step toward the company's goal. It is important to understand that this growth is also not solely a result of relationships with microfinance providers. In order to sustain its business, FINO has reached out to a new customer base that includes banks, insurance providers, and the Indian government. Many of the million clients on the FINO platform are recipients of government payouts and subsidies, rather than microfinance customers. The FINO platform provides a lower-cost, more efficient way for the government to provide these benefits to its citizens.

Products provided on the centralized FINO platform include savings accounts, loan accounts, remittances, recurring deposits, and fixed deposits. The FINO smart cards enable the customers to use a FINO biometric electronic-funds-transfer-at-point-of-sale (EFTPOS) device to perform all of the functions related to these accounts: looking up balances, transferring funds, making deposits, and making withdrawals.

Services offered by FINO include customer enrollment, account hosting, and help desk. The customer enrollment process involves proper customer identification followed by issuance of a smart card with a photo. The FINO system is built atop a core banking solution from i-flex, which provides all of the data storage and processing power for calculations and reports. I-flex is a major banking application that handles many types of transactions and connects to external systems. By linking the modalities offered by a mobile-network-enabled EFTPOS on the front end with the capabilities of a core banking solution on the back end, FINO is leveraging the strengths of these two technologies. Finally, FINO offers Help Desk 24X6 for resolving critical business issues. The help desk can work to resolve any issue involving FINO, thus providing a single point of contact for all issues.

Lessons learned in FINO's experience include the following:

- *Wholesale lenders should not be overly involved.* Many of the MFIs in India considered ICICI too close to the solution, raising issues of independence and potential conflict of interest, as ICICI held much of the debt for these organizations. The MFIs feared that over time, ICICI Bank would be able to establish direct relationships with their clients and the MFIs would become irrelevant.

- *Existing investment in technology must be accounted for in terms of switching costs.* The leading microfinance players in India had already made substantial investments in their MIS platforms and technology teams. As such, they were reluctant to migrate to a new platform and away from systems that had been designed for their businesses and that were working well. Until there was at least one microfinance provider successfully using the solution, others were reluctant to sign up. The cheief executive officers (CEOs) wanted to see an operational example of how the solution would work. This presented a bit of a chicken-and-egg situation for FINO: how to convince the first MFI to participate if each of them was waiting to see a successful implementation?

- *Cost is prohibitive for smaller organizations.* Initial cost projections for the solution were a hindrance to other potential customers. This was particularly true among the smaller MFIs, which had established their own, unsophisticated technology solutions and had a very small staff. In some cases, these smaller institutions had an information technology (IT) staff of only one person. Thus, small MFIs felt that their current IT costs were miniscule to nonexistent. Without a strong incentive for participation, they had no reason to make what to them would be a high technology investment.

Latin American Financial Grid (IBM)
Based on an examination of the unmet need for financial services, IBM Global Services is in the early stages of planning for a Latin America–wide strategy for a centralized ICT platform for microfinance. The platform envisioned includes a model of service delivery, hosting, and tailored functionality. Figure 4.2 describes the initiative.

The hub is expected to be located in Mexico and serve all of MFIs in Spanish-speaking Latin America with a Web-based solution. In its analysis, IBM identified 358,580,000 people in the region who are unbanked, providing it with a significant potential market (IBM 2008).

Emerging themes from IBM's experience include the following:

- *Connectivity must be a focus.* Connectivity, in fact is the key theme to emerge from this effort, as it is a requirement for participation.
- *Create a structure that includes governance, MFI onboarding, and regulatory and compliance,* as well as the anticipated technological components. These are important for the overall success of the implementation.
- *Include fulfillment in the concept from the beginning.* In its presentations, IBM identifies the local provider that ensures that the implementation goes smoothly.

RSI: Spain
Rural Servicios Informáticos (RSI) was founded in 1986 by a small group of rural savings banks that were pioneers in today's widespread policy for outsourcing services. RSI opted to concentrate its investment capacity on creating a common database, designed to centralize its operational support

Figure 4.2   The Latin America Initiative

a processing hub provides a shared infrastructure and services platform that facilitates the integration of MFIs and poor communities into the overall financial ecosystem

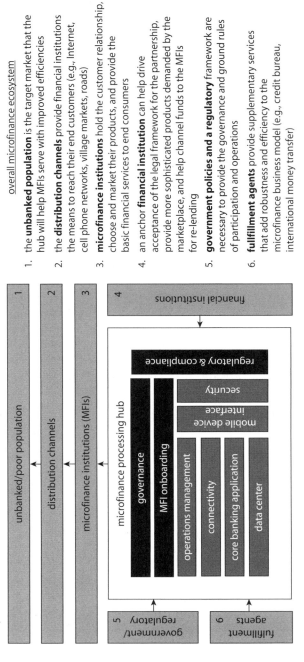

overall microfinance ecosystem

1. the **unbanked population** is the target market that the hub will help MFIs serve with improved efficiencies

2. the **distribution channels** provide financial institutions the means to reach their end customers (e.g., Internet, cell phone networks, village markets, roads)

3. **microfinance institutions** hold the customer relationship, choose and market their products, and provide the basic financial services to end consumers

4. an anchor **financial institution** can help drive acceptance of the legal framework for the partnership, provide more sophisticated products demanded by the marketplace, and help channel funds to the MFIs for re-lending

5. **government policies and a regulatory** framework are necessary to provide the governance and ground rules of participation and operations

6. **fulfillment agents** provide supplementary services that add robustness and efficiency to the microfinance business model (e.g., credit bureau, international money transfer)

Source: IBM Financial Services 2008.

61

services in a common operational data center. The board is composed of representatives from the following institutions: Banco Cooperativo Español (one), Rural IT Services GDM (one), biggest cooperatives (five), and small and medium cooperatives (two).

As a private company, RSI has had to reduce its costs in order to be self-sufficient and to provide better returns to its partners each year. RSI's prices are based on a fixed transaction cost: the more transactions you make, the more you pay. Each cooperative buys its own hardware but it must be approved by Rural IT Services in order to maintain standards across the members. RSI uses its own software, which it sold in 2001 to Temenos and is now called Temenos Core Banking, which Bansefi also uses.

This platform is being used by the Spanish government's regulatory entity, Banco de España. The regulatory authority has established an office within RSI that helps it access all the required information that a regulator would need from a supervised entity, an agreement that was established through a memorandum of understanding. The entity provides a password to the regulator to permit access to the information. In this way, the MFI regulatory authority ensures that data quality is maintained for each entity and that the operational procedures of the MFI, backup measures, security, and the disaster recovery plan are all up to the required legal standards. From this collaboration, the regulator is assured that the layout of the data in the system is the same for all the reporting entities and therefore an onsite audit would concentrate only on deviations from this data layout.

Lessons learned from RSI's experience include the following:

- *Developing a new system takes a long time.* It took RSI more than nine years to implement the project.
- *At the time when this intervention was begun, the communication infrastructure in Spain was not as good as it today.* The systems operated offline, indicating that the connectivity levels in Bangladesh are much better as we begin to implement any ICT interventions. This means that one does not have to spend so much time either developing systems or worrying about connectivity issues.
- *Success of this kind of intervention depends on transaction volumes.* In the case of Spain, the break-even point was reached after four years. This was after 60 MFIs were fully utilizing the system. This intervention demonstrates the fact that shareholders of such an investment can be MFIs and banks, who are the eventual users of the system.

FIDUCIA: Germany

The cooperative banks developed their own technological platform and created a company called FIDUCIA to operate it. Today, FIDUCIA is one of the 10 leading IT service providers in Germany. Its services range from strategic IT consulting to development and implementation of IT solutions to technical and application-centered operations in professional computer centers. The FIDUCIA Group, with headquarters in Karlsruhe, also serves as the IT competence center.

FIDUCIA's largest customer group consists of 800 people's banks and rural credit cooperatives (Volksbanken and Raiffeisenbanken), making FIDUCIA the largest IT service provider to cooperative banks. FIDUCIA's core banking system, Agree, is currently used by this set of institutions and, as a result, it is one of the leading banking systems in Germany.

FIDUCIA's state-of-the-art IT solutions meet the high demands of its customers in regard to availability (time to market) and operating economy. Once availability is defined, the focus in developing and providing application systems is on maximum data security and protection—even where large volumes of data are involved. Through its comprehensive approach to solutions, FIDUCIA increases the efficiency of customer processes, thereby strengthening the market position of its customers.

Lessons learned from FIDUCIA's experience include the following:

- *As in the case of RSI, it takes time to develop a sustainable ICT platform.* There are fixed, initial costs that have to be covered. Initial subscribers might not be able to pay the full price. As transactions and the number of entities increase so is their contribution in terms of paying up to the full price of utilizing the platform.
- *The two data centers that process MFIs transactions in Germany are likely to merge.* Such a move would take advantage of economies of scale.
- *It is imperative that the management of the entity responsible for the operations of the platform is of high quality and that the biggest MFI does not manage the central business unit.*
- Advisory committees work very well in this type of company.

Metavante: United States

Banking is one of the largest industries in the United States, and technological advancement has become the discerning factor in terms of which institutions can provide the services customers need. Small and regional banks, in particular, are seeking systems that will automate some of their operations, so that they can focus all their energies and money on winning new customers and making sure that customers' needs are fulfilled.

Metavante, headquartered in Milwaukee, Wisconsin, has grown rapidly and is already registered on the New York Stock Exchange. The company delivers banking and payments technologies to more than 8,000 financial services firms and businesses worldwide. Metavante products and services drive account processing for deposit, loan and trust systems, image-based and conventional check processing, electronic funds transfer, consumer healthcare payments, business transformation services, and payment network solutions (including the NYCE Network, a leading ATM/PIN debit network). Metavante charges fees according to the volume of transactions.

Lessons learned from Metavante's experience include the following:

- *Providing a centralized platform that interfaces with small MFIs and banks can save those institutions, as well as government and regulatory entities, a significant amount of money.* In Metavante's case, the company also provides assurance to the government and regulators that the system complies with international standards for such operations.

Bansefi: Mexico

Bansefi, created as a national savings program to enable the mobilization of savings in Mexico, is a development bank with a market presence in all Mexican states. In 2001, the Mexican government promulgated a law to regulate MFI activities, and Bansefi was tasked with supporting this regulatory compliance. A technology project was launched shortly thereafter to assist the MFIs with compliance with the law, help them reduce their operational costs, and assist them in offering new products and services to their clients. A centralized platform, Bansefi's main objective was to enable the Mexican government to properly supervise the MFIs' public savings programs.

Bansefi's plan was to include the more than 600 MFIs that collectively serve more than 4 million customers. The centralized technology platform was intended to scale to 20 million customers (the number of potential MFI customers in Mexico) in order to reach the unbanked population across the country and thus serve the public policy aims of financial inclusion and efficiency.

The project installed a centralized ICT platform based on IBM mainframe machines and using software that supported the more than 5 million customers. Because of the need for centralized data and the lack of connectivity in many remote areas without telephone lines, the telecommunications strategy included infrastructure through satellite communications and antenna devices.

Issues with the project surfaced during implementation, however, as each MFI had different products, different procedures, and differing levels of skills. Moreover, the Mexican government began promulgating additional rules related to the law, which proved unpopular and tainted the overall impression of the Centralized ICT platform. The MFI's had the impression that the platform was being used to enforce new regulation.

As part of implementation, the project included training, procedural changes, and data migration. The migration of historical data was problematic, however, because of many errors in the structure and completeness of the data.

In the end, MFI entities still participating in Bansefi have seen a number of improvements, as they have been able to free people up from back-office activities and apply them to customer services, keep prices for their products low, obtain access to data online, and comply with regulatory reports. The Mexican government itself is pleased because of the transparency of transactions. Customers are also empowered by having access to the entire financial service system, for example via ATMs and EFTPOS devices in other localities.

Lessons learned from Bansefi's experience include the following:

- *Have a clear understanding of the MFI procedures and technological ability prior to commencing the project.* While training can assist implementation, project managers must ground the project in the reality of the field. That reality may mean that MFIs use inconsistent procedures and have low exposure to technology.

- *Undertake data migration only when it makes sense.* Lack of good data structures was not obvious to the MFIs, which claimed their data were clean. Because many MFIs were not familiar with good data practices, they assumed that their data were adequate, when such data were not. Data migration is almost always a difficult process, and the cost of data migration should be balanced against the benefit of specific use cases and reports that can be generated.

- *Do not embed regulatory compliance into an effort to develop a technology platform.* By doing so, the Bansefi technology project became synonymous with government regulation. This negatively affected the project by causing MFIs to pull out of the effort. If the project had first developed the common platform and then worked on the regulatory aspects, it would likely have been more successful in maintaining the interest of MFIs.

Other Efforts Under Way

Though information about it is not publicly available, a new initiative to provide a shared back-office solution for MFIs in Africa has been initiated by CARE in partnership with IBM. The initiative is grounded in the fact that most MFIs in Africa do not have an information system and most Africans do not have access to financial services.

In Indonesia, a new initiative by Mercy Corps links the creation of a funding apex bank (bank of banks) with developing a standard back-office solution for data management at its client MFIs. The new bank will provide wholesale loans to MFIs and other small financial institutions in Indonesia, in order to take advantage of a huge market opportunity of 235 million people, the vast majority of whom are unbanked.

These efforts illustrate that in markets with existing software-solution providers, there remains a need for a common platform that is affordable and easy to implement at a range of institutions.

CHAPTER 5

Creating an Enabling Environment: Policy and Regulations

This chapter describes and examines the key features of the policy- and regulatory-enabling environment across the financial, microfinance, and information technology sectors that will impact the envisaged centralized ICT platform. It considers the impact of current and future regulations on the platform, and outlines a number of enabling areas that would further enhance the benefits expected from the implementation of a centralized ICT platform.

Regulations were examined to determine if there was anything that could preclude the development of a centralized ICT platform, and to point out potential areas of challenge. A scan of the regulatory environment was conducted to inform this section and to identify any glaring challenges.

From a regulatory perspective, the proposed centralized ICT platform is at the nexus of three sectors: microfinance, ICT, and financial services. The platform aims to leverage each of them to extend the delivery of financial applications to the underserved population of Bangladesh. Financial sector and ICT regulations are therefore reviewed here to identify any roadblocks to nonbank financial transactions.

Ensuring that the technology platform can be operated by nontelecommunications operators, in a regulatory environment where electronic transactions are provisioned and consumers' data privacy protected, is just as important as microfinance and financial-sector considerations. After reviewing whether the microfinance and financial sector regulatory space is conducive to the proposed microfinance platform, the report examines regulations related to telecommunications, information technology (IT), cyber law, and security.

Enabling Microfinance Regulations

While the microcredit regulatory function in Bangladesh would benefit from the ongoing capacity building and a relicensing process, there do not seem to be any current microfinance regulations that would interfere with the development of a centralized ICT platform. Since regulations in the financial and microfinance sectors are still in flux, it is recommended that the development of new policies into law be followed closely.

Microcredit Regulatory Authority (MRA)

At present, Grameen Bank is the only formal financial institution in Bangladesh established under a special law. Rapid growth of the microfinance sector after 1990 in terms of outreach and product development encouraged the government to form the Microfinance Research and Reference Unit (MRRU) in 2000 under the supervision of a National Steering Committee (NSC), which, headed by the governor of the Bangladesh Bank, formulates guidelines and suggests a regulatory framework for the microfinance sector. Initially, the NSC prepared a set of guidelines that were implemented by the MRRU. Those guidelines helped the sector to prepare for a future regulatory environment that would be in place and to build up a friendly communication between the sector and the policy makers. At a later stage, the NSC prepared a draft regulatory framework after consultation with the sector representatives and submitted it to the government. That draft was the basis of the Microcredit Regulatory Authority Act, which the government passed in July 2006. Under this law, the government has established the separate Microcredit Regulatory Authority (MRA) and named its board of directors, with the governor of the Bangladesh Bank as the chairperson.

Before the Microcredit Regulatory Authority Act, MFIs were unregulated. Under the new law, all active MFIs had to apply for a license from the MRA before the end of February 2007. Of 4,000 applications from NGOs and MFIs, 374 licenses had been granted as of October 4, 2009. According to the law, all institutions with microcredit operations should separate their financial operations from other development works and keep their accounts separate. The MRA has been given power to monitor and supervise all the licensed MFIs, and no unlicensed institution will be allowed to provide microfinance services. The MRA also has the power to prepare detailed rules related to the operations of MFIs, including conditions related to spending any income, areas of operation, guidelines of internal and external auditing of accounts, collection of deposits, and use of earned profit. The MRA is also mandated to take punitive measures if any institution does not comply with any of the provisions of the law.

Preparation of detailed regulations based on the Microcredit Regulatory Authority Act is ongoing. Finalization of the regulations, which was previously planned for submission to the board of the MRA by the end of June 2008, has been delayed to allow for incorporation of feedback from targeted consultations with NGOs, policy makers, and others. The regulations will take effect after clearance from the MRA board. The regulations do not provide guidelines on linkages between commercial banks and MFIs, leaving gray areas regarding the regulatory field between banks and MFIs.

Enabling Financial Sector Regulations and Applications

The regulatory environment as it relates to enabling applications for the centralized ICT platform was also considered. Currently, no regulations interfere with the applications that would be carried over the platform. However, current legislation prescribes nonbank agents to provide key financial services applications and may call for linkages between MFIs, commercial banks, and other operators for these services.

Central Bank Policies

While the commercial banking sector in Bangladesh has been deregulated, the Bangladesh Bank, as the central bank, has legal authority to supervise and regulate the banks. It performs the traditional central banking roles of note issuance and of being banker to the government and banks. It also formulates and implements monetary policy, manages foreign exchange reserves, and supervises banks and nonbank financial institutions. Prudential regulations that it imposes on commercial banks include minimum capital requirements, limits on loan concentration and insider borrowing, and guidelines for asset classification and income recognition. The Bangladesh Bank has the power to impose penalties for noncompliance and also to intervene in the management of a bank if serious problems arise. The Bangladesh Bank is currently encouraging linkages between commercial banks and MFIs through the business financial working group of the existing Better Business Forum.

Bank Licensing

The Bank Company Act of 1991 empowers the Bangladesh Bank to issue licenses to carry out banking business in Bangladesh. The Act requires a bank to seek approval from the Bangladesh Bank by November of each year to set up new branches, with response, in principle, from the Bangladesh Bank by March of the subsequent year and the kick-off of licensing application process thereafter. The Bangladesh Bank recognizes that expansion of bank branches in the rural areas is a profitable venture and would contribute to increasing banks' competitive capacity, particularly in the context of delivering increasing levels of remittances. Consequently, a requirement to obtain Bangladesh Bank approval is the rollout of one rural area branch for every four urban branches. As of November 2007, the total number of branches of all banks stood at 6,654, an increase from 6,596 in June 2007 and 6,425 in June 2006. Between June 2006 and November 2007, private commercial banks opened 90 new branches in rural areas and 122 in urban areas. In 2008, the Bangladesh Bank authorized 138 bank branches, of which 79 new rural branches were licensed.

Bank Deposit Insurance

The Bank Deposit Insurance Act of 2000 mandates that all commercial banks operating in Bangladesh, including foreign banks and specialized banks, follow the Deposit Insurance Scheme (DIS), although nonbanking financial institutions remain out of the purview of DIS. Under the scheme, a depositor is insured on losses up to Tk 100,000, to be paid out within 90 days of liquidation of a bank.

Risk-based premium rates were introduced in 2007, with problem banks required to pay a 0.09 percent premium and all other private banks a 0.07 percent premium. The collected premium is deposited in the Deposit Insurance Trust Fund account maintained by the Bangladesh Bank.

In order to improve the effectiveness of DIS in reducing systemic risk, the Bangladesh Bank has advised banks to increase public awareness of the existence and scope of DIS through display notification in all banks.

IT Security Standards

The Guideline on Information & Communication Technology for Scheduled Banks and Financial Institutions, issued by the Bangladesh

Bank in 2005, set minimum security standards for banks and financial institutions and covers all activities and operations required to ensure data security, including facility design, physical security, network security, disaster recovery and business continuity planning, use of hardware and software, data disposal, and protection of copyrights and other intellectual property rights.

Banks are also required to submit compliance reports, and the Bangladesh Bank monitors the progress of implementation of these security standards through its onsite inspection teams during routine inspections.

Credit Information Bureau Application[1]

The Credit Information Bureau (CIB), set up by the Bangladesh Bank in 1992, suffers from narrow scope and limited accessibility due to the manual nature of data management. For example, banks communicate with the Bangladesh Bank largely by sending information on diskettes.

Participating members currently include 49 banks and 27 financial institutions. Every institution having a minimum loan size of Tk 50,000 is required to submit its borrower records, including details on the outstanding loan amount, disbursement, recovery, type and maturity of loan, type of collateral, and guarantees securing the loan.

Access to credit information varies across different groups. The Bangladesh Bank management has access to all information; banks and financial institutions have access to credit reports that contain detailed information but exclude the names of the lending institutions; and government departments only have access to reports that reveal the default status of the borrower. Additionally, borrowers have a unique rating, which includes information on all loans taken from the financial system and is available for distribution to all financial institutions.

With assistance from the U.K. Department for International Development (DFID), the Bangladesh Bank is now in the process of developing an online CIB. The Bangladesh Bank is also committed to upgrading and automating the CIB with support from DFID and the International Finance Corporation (IFC). The scope of the project is to equip the CIB with resources necessary to be consistent with international standards and meet the demands of the financial sector. The new CIB application system will both streamline the collection of data from banks/financial institutions and consolidate the collected data into an expanded central database, with tools that will allow greater through-put and expanded analytical capabilities. To select the vendor, an international tendering process was initiated in March 2008 and the vendor is at the final stages of gathering the requirements from the CIB team at Bangladesh Bank. The official handover of the complete solution is expected to be at the end of October 2010.

Banking Services Applications

Remittance services. Only licensed and supervised banks and their branches and overseas centers are allowed to receive remittances in Bangladesh. Efforts have been undertaken to expand the outreach of remittance services to rural areas and remote locations in the country in which the population has no means to receive its remittances. Banks are allowed to engage MFIs only as the delivery leg of local currency in the process of migrant remittances. Accordingly, some banks have usefully engaged the extensive branch networks of microfinance NGOs in the delivery of remittances to recipients in very remote rural locations—for example, Western Union transfers by BRAC Bank (using BRAC branches as a rural distribution network), ATMs at MFI point-of-sale (POS) terminals in 300 TMSS branches. Under mutual agreements, banks also deliver funds via interbank branch transfers in locations where they do not have branches. While authorities have set 48-hour and 72-hour remittance delivery time standards, respectively, for urban and rural areas, compliance with the rural standard is largely unmet.

Domestic private money exchanges and money changers and MFIs are not allowed to deal directly in or handle foreign remittances. The Bangladesh Postal Department is the only nonbank financial institution allowed to channel remittances, which it does through various agreements with counterparts in different countries through which migrants can send money via international money orders. Ultimately, remittances inflows are still channeled through the banks.

E-Payment and Mobile Payment System Regulations

Currently, nonbank financial institutions (including MFIs) cannot be licensed to operate points of sale for the delivery of financial services. However, a few initiatives in remittances services attempt to increase financial infrastructure delivery despite these constraints: a bank, for example, can ask the Bangladesh Bank for permission to involve an NGO in the delivery process, as a point of sale. The NGO is therefore allowed to act as a channel for remittance delivery. However, under the current regulatory environment, the NGO is currently bound by an exclusivity partnership with a bank. The preclusion from licensing NGOs as payment system providers limits the opportunities of multiple remittance delivery through one nonfinancial institution's network. Similarly, telecommunications operators cannot currently hold money and loan installments on mobile phones.

The Bangladesh Bank has been empowered to issue regulations on payment systems and is currently attempting to address some of these constraints through finalizing regulations for e-payment systems. These regulations include provisions to facilitate m-payments. The final draft regulations incorporate feedback received through a consultation process and have now been submitted to the governor of the Bangladesh Bank, after clearance from the National Payment Council. To address other issues pertaining to the granting of financial services providers' licenses, the Bangladesh Bank plans to issue payment-system provider regulations once the regulations for e-payments are finalized.

Scheduled banks are rapidly adopting modern and innovative technology-driven products, including debit, credit, and other ATM cards. In recent years, banks have put emphasis on improving the speed and convenience of transactions through introducing ATM, POS, online, Internet, telebanking, and Society for Worldwide Interbank Financial Telecommunication (SWIFT) capabilities.

Traditionally, scheduled banks provided cash transaction facilities through their branches. Over the past decade, this activity has been extended with adoption of ATM booths and POS terminals in different urban areas. However, as an important means of payment and transactions, the use of checks is also widespread. The Bangladesh Bank and Sonali Bank Ltd. act as the clearinghouses to clear and settle checks, drafts, and payment orders in domestic currency. Drafts (foreign direct deposits), checks, bills, and payment orders in foreign currency are cleared and settled through the scheduled banks' foreign currency clearing account maintained with the Bangladesh Bank.

Conventional banks still use telegraphic transfer, mail transfer, payment order, and demand draft for transferring funds between locations; these are tedious and time-consuming processes. With modern technology, the same functions are performed through individual bank online networks, Internet, and SWIFT, all of which provide instant transactional facility.

In October 2009, Bangladesh Bank approved the launch of an electronic pre-paid card system, which includes a mobile payment option (*The Daily Star* 2009). Under this scheme, customers can deposit and withdraw cash directly from ATMs and other channels through the card's PIN access and the system also allows an authorized user to transact by mobile. A local bank (Trust Bank Ltd.) has been authorized to be the settlement bank for this digital money transfer scheme and it is hoped to be implemented within six months. Furthermore, another local bank (Dhaka Bank) was granted authority to disburse foreign remittance through mobile operator Banglalink's outlets.

Interbank Payment Systems Applications

Clearing of accounts and transactions is currently not automated in Bangladesh, leading to long delays (one to two weeks) in formal payment in interbank systems. With the exception of two ATM cash networks (Q-cash ATM network), there are no ATM networks.

Under a recent initiative, however, several banks have formed a company that will set up 505 ATMs across the country over the next three years. The hope is that this process will bring more people under an electronic transaction system, as more than 60 percent of the ATMs will be set up in rural areas. Besides ATMs, some 10,000 POS centers, 950,000 debit cards, and more than 2 million prepaid cards will be marketed under the project by 2010. As of October 2007, there were only 438 ATMs, 10,526 POS centers, 770,000 debit cards, and 30,000 credit cards issued by all banks in the country.

As part of a three-year project under implementation since November 2006, with DFID support, the Bangladesh Bank is the anchor for a payment systems project aimed at (1) establishing an automated clearinghouse (ACH) for payment systems and enhancing the present enabling legal environment to operate the ACH, (2) setting up a challenge fund for private enterprises to stimulate innovation in the delivery and use of migrant remittances and (3) building an awareness of these activities. In the initial stage, the ACH will enable a network of 49 banks to perform the task of electronic fund transfer and automated check processing. Two centralized clearing houses will be set up in Dhaka and Chittagong, in addition to a disaster recovery center for backup. A vendor agreement has been signed and the systems are expected to be operational in the second half of 2009.

Enabling ICT and Electronic Data Regulations

Regulations related to telecommunications, IT, cyber law, and security would also have an impact on the proposed microfinance technology platform. Although the microfinance sector in Bangladesh suffers from fragmented regulatory oversight, none of the regulations and policies articulated below would interfere with the centralized ICT platform. In fact, all the policies appear to be strongly supportive of the extension of IT, universal access (including reach into rural areas), and improvement of government access to data and linkages. All of these elements are a core part of the value proposition of the centralized ICT platform.

Fragmented Regulatory Oversight

The telecom/ICT environment is fragmented, complicating the convergence of ICT toward a unified voice and data environment. While the Bangladesh Telecommunication Regulatory Commission (BTRC) supervises telecommunications and ICT, content and media services do not fall under its purview. Internet content is currently under the purview of the two broadcasting regulators for television and radio.

BTRC was established by the Bangladesh Telecommunications Act of 2001 as an independent commission to regulate the sector. BTRC is responsible for licensing operators and ensuring compliance with license terms and conditions, managing the radio spectrum, ensuring technical compatibility and effective interconnection between service providers, monitoring carrier quality of service, approving tariffs, and providing equipment type approval.

Broadband License Issuance: An Enabler of New Applications

Ineffective radio spectrum management was identified as a significant problem by private sector investors, and in the past BTRC has not been able to effectively manage the radio spectrum or reap fiscal benefits from the optimal use of this national resource. However, BTRC granted three WiMAX (Worldwide Interoperability for Microwave Access) licenses in September 2008[2] in addition to one licensed to state-run Bangladesh Telecommunications Company Limited (BTCL). BTRC also had plans to issue four third-generation (3G) licenses by January 2009. WiMAX and 3G technologies offer broadband speed that will allow the rollout of more bandwidth-intensive services, e-commerce or m-commerce, for example, which was not possible under 2.5G licenses. Operators such as GrameenPhone have been waiting to obtain 3G licenses to commercialize e-commerce and m-wallet services. Financial transaction services now allowed by 3G include balance checks, deposits, and transfers (including remittances).

Open Licensing

Bangladesh has adopted an open licensing regime for services by Internet service providers, satellite phone companies, and public switched telephone network services. An open auction system has been introduced as one of the mechanisms for granting licenses, particularly for voice-over-Internet-protocol (VoIP) and network services. In view of the limited service spectrum, granting of licenses for cellular mobile phone service is done through competitive bidding procedure.

National Telecommunications Policy of 1998

The National Telecommunications Policy of 1998 was formulated to ensure the orderly and rapid growth of telecommunications services, both in quality and quantity, and the use of telecommunications technology, recognizing competition and private participation as means of promoting improved sector performance.

At the time of the policy, the government also withdrew all import duties and value-added tax on computer hardware and software and offered corporate tax exemption facility for IT companies through 2008. The fiscal year 2008/09 budget extended this facility for a further three years.

National ICT Policy of 2002

This policy, currently under review in a Better Business Forum exercise, aims at building an ICT-driven nation to facilitate empowerment of people and sustainable economic development by using the ICT infrastructure for human resources development, governance, e-commerce, banking, public utility services, and other ICT-enabled services. The policy has been conducive to opening up participation in the telecom sector in order to establish connectivity across the country. However, in terms of its overarching vision, a comprehensive roadmap has not been developed, leading to piecemeal efforts in implementation.

Cyber Legislation

The ICT Act of 2006 is aimed at facilitating e-communications and eliminating barriers to e-commerce by providing legal recognition and acceptance of e-signatures and e-records for filing, issue, grant, receipt, or payment.

However, while acceptance and processing of documents and monetary transactions in electronic format is increasingly encouraged, the act, in and of itself, does not compel any government ministry, agency, or department to accept, issue, create, retain, or preserve any document in the form of e-records or process any monetary transaction (including e-commerce, e-banking, and credit card transactions) in electronic form.

The Controller of ICT Certifying Authorities (CICA) will be responsible for regulating ICT Certifying Authorities' activities by issuing licenses, setting standards and conditions by which the industry must abide, and specifying the form and content of e-signature certification. The CICA will also be the repository of all e-signature certificates. Although the establishment of CICA was to be within 90 days of the act's promulgation, it has yet to be implemented by the government.

The ICT Act of 2006 also establishes cyber laws, detailing offences, punishment, penalties, and adjudication and calls for the creation of one or more cyber tribunals and cyber appeals tribunals to deal with crimes committed that fall under the purview of this act. Other acts that will be amended as a result of this one include the Penal Code of 1860, Evidence Act of 1872, Bankers' Books Evidence Act of 1891, and Bangladesh Bank Order of 1972. The ICT Act of 2006 will override inconsistencies in any other laws in force.

International Long Distance Telecommunications Services Policy of 2007

Following the mushrooming of VoIP services and the subsequent government crackdown on illegal units, BTRC recently formulated the International Long Distance Telecommunications Services (ILDTS) Policy to facilitate, liberalize, and legitimize ILDTS, including VoIP services, with a focus on providing low-cost international telecommunications services, encouraging local businesses and enterprises in the telecom sector, and encouraging next-generation network technology.

The policy provides for three private international gateway (IGW) operators in addition to the government-owned Bangladesh Telegraph and Telephone Board (BTTB). The operators will be required to be located in Dhaka and will provide international voice call services, including VoIP termination and origination. The policy also provides for two interconnection exchange (ICX) operators, each with three ICXs, in addition to BTTB, which, depending on traffic volume, could later be expanded under BTRC guidance. There will also be two Internet exchanges (IXs) under one operator, in addition to existing international exchanges. These, too, may be expanded in future.

The license-awarding procedure maintains that IGW, ICX, and IX licenses will be issued only to Bangladeshi entities. No foreign entities or nonresident Bangladeshi entities will be eligible to be owners, directors, shareholders, investors, or partners of these licensee entities. A single business entity will be allowed to obtain only one license of IGW, ICX, or IX category, and operators already holding any license from BTRC will not be eligible. Furthermore, all financial transactions will have to be made through scheduled banks in Bangladesh. Licenses will be awarded through open auction. Different tariff structures will be set by BTRC for voice and data services and will be revised periodically. Following auctions in 2008, BTRC has awarded licenses for IGW, ICX, and IX services.

Guidelines on Call Center Licensing of 2008

BTRC has recently invited applications to grant licenses for call centers, hosted call centers (HCCs), and HCC service providers, to be provided on a first-come, first-served basis. Five-year licenses will be given to individuals, partnerships, or companies/joint ventures registered and formed in Bangladesh. The guidelines state that foreign equity will be limited to a maximum 45 percent for call centers, HCCs, and HCC service providers, while for nonresident Bangladeshis, the maximum limit will be 70 percent. For captive international call centers, 100 percent foreign direct investment is permissible, although foreign investors must bring in all equity financing from overseas. Furthermore, employment of foreign expatriates will be limited to 10 percent after the first year of operation.

Other Regulation

Both BTRC and the Bangladesh Bank have the power under their respective acts to protect consumers for all regulated areas. A consumer protection act for all sectors of the economy is at the final stage of being vetted.

Going Forward

While no microfinance, financial sector, or ICT regulations were found to prevent the operationalization of the proposed centralized ICT platform, the regulatory space would benefit from further embracing and facilitating new financial sector infrastructure through the centralized ICT platform, with the aim of achieving universal access to formal finance in Bangladesh. Given that it was not developed with the convergence of telecommunications and finance in mind, existing regulation may leave gaps and ambiguities. However, it is important to bear in mind that any regulatory framework in this field should be proportionate in terms of giving space for new innovations to scale up safely, such as by allowing scope for different means of compliance, so that market participants are not unduly restricted from launching new financial products and services.

Going forward, several regulatory areas could be addressed to leverage and increase the benefits of the centralized ICT platform in terms of information sharing, linkages with the financial sector, increase in reach, and product range.

Strengthening of Microfinance Regulation

Improved monitoring and evaluation and capacity building of the microfinance regulator, in particular, has the potential to strengthen microfinance regulation. Increased capacity of the regulator will be critical to leverage the opportunities of more timely, systematic, and accurate information that the centralized platform will bring about. Often times, there is a temptation to underestimate the challenge of supervision, with the result that regulation is not enforced, which can be worse than no regulation at all. Supervision of microfinance, particularly portfolio testing, requires techniques and skills that are different from those used to supervise commercial banks. Supervisory staff will thus need to be trained and, to some extent, specialized, in order to deal effectively with MFIs and intervene strategically to correct the challenges faced in the industry.

Direct Engagement among Players

Given that the centralized ICT platform ties together three distinct sectors, establishing direct engagement among policy makers, regulators, and interested industry players will be especially important as regulatory authorities become acquainted with industry actors they do not traditionally regulate, such as banking regulators and supervisors and mobile network operators.

Enabling Regulation for Nonbank Financial Services

Regulation in Bangladesh continues to constraint the emergence of banking through nonbank operators, including through MFIs. Without addressing this issue through making the necessary changes in the current regulatory framework, MFIs would not be able to derive the full benefits of a centralized platform by becoming payment system providers not held to exclusive partnerships with banks. Similarly, while recent technology license development in Bangladesh creates promising developments for the delivery of financial services via mobile banking platforms, current regulations do not allow nonbank agents to provide financial services. It is recommended that the upcoming payment system provider regulations allow for nonbank financial services provision in order for MFIs to offer value-added products such as remittance services and mobile banking.

Consumer Protection Regulations

Both banking and mobile communications are fundamentally about information. As such, financial consumer protection issues should be a main concern. The electronic storage and transmittal of minutely detailed electronic records about MFIs, their customers and their transactions, as made possible by the centralized platform, increase the importance of consumer data privacy and security protection. Simple but robust mechanisms could be created, covering problems with POS operators, redress of grievances through a financial sector ombudsman, price transparency, and consumer data privacy. A combination of regulation (such as the consumer protection currently being vetted) and awareness campaigns targeting MFIs and clients to inform them about the protections afforded by regulation will be critical for the adoption of the centralized ICT platform and the value-added services it will provide.

Fraud and Financial Crime Prevention

The area of antifraud and financial crime regulation will need to be adequate to address abuse by any of MFIs connected to the centralized platform. In return, the platform would provide a channel for reaching anti–money laundering (AML) standards. The Money Laundering Prevention Act 2002, which has been further updated under the Money Laundering Prevention Ordinance 2007,[3] is the primary AML legislation in Bangladesh. A U.S. Department of State (2007) report finds that the AML regime in Bangladesh needs to be further strengthened. At present, however, customer identification requirements are difficult to enforce, as most customers do not have passports or other forms of identity. Transaction records are also manually maintained due to lack of technology, although head offices in urban areas are moving towards computerization. In addition, Bangladesh does not have provisions for safe harbor or banker negligence accountability. The centralized ICT platform could help better serve AML objectives by helping to monitor electronic transactions and improving data availability for law enforcement.

Notes

1. Information in this section is from World Bank (2008).
2. BRAC Bdmail Network, BanglaLion Communications, and Augere Wireless Broadband Bangladesh were the three private operators selected by BTRC for a WiMAX license via an auction process.
3. The Ordinance was promulgated under the caretaker government regime and is now awaiting ratification by parliament.

CHAPTER 6

Technology Design

This chapter describes the building blocks required, from a technology standpoint, to establish a centralized ICT platform in Bangladesh. Such building blocks are needed at the host institution serving as the center of the microfinance industry of Bangladesh, in each of the offices of the participating microfinance institutions (MFIs), and among the loan officers. All MFIs would connect with the center using electronic communication links.

While the design of the technology solution would follow the requirements identified in previous chapters, this chapter covers the details of how the proposed technology solution would meet the needs of the various stakeholders in the microfinance industry in Bangladesh. It outlines key functional and operational standards that must be met in order to ensure that the platform is capable of serving a variety of stakeholders within the microfinance industry of Bangladesh, while also addressing each MFI's individual needs.

The goal of the technology design of the centralized ICT platform is to provide a simple solution that is capable of serving the entire microfinance industry of Bangladesh at an affordable price. The platform must cater to the variety of stakeholders in the industry yet adapt to the individual needs of the primary stakeholders, namely the MFIs.

Models of Technology Deployment

There are several ways by which technology can be deployed in MFIs across Bangladesh: (1) individually, on an institution-by-institution basis; (2) wholesale, with a common platform; or (3) with common industry standards, as some sophisticated industries do.

The "Microsoft Office Model"

The "Microsoft Office model" is the most common way by which technology is deployed—for each user or each institution. Under this model, each uses a common application, such as Microsoft Office, on the computer. The user saves all work on the hard drive of the computer. No two users are able to look at each other's work, and users exchange information in the form of e-mail. The Microsoft Office model works well for individuals and helps increase their productivity. But the model does not lend itself to a large community in which users have need to constantly exchange information with one another. Under the Microsoft Office model, it also becomes difficult to introduce technology within a large community of users. Maintaining technology for the entire community of users is even more difficult.

The "Gmail Model"

The "Gmail model" is the new way by which technology is deployed on a wholesale basis, using a common platform. In practice, variations of the Gmail model are also common. According to this model, each user has a computer and connects to an online application via a user account (using a username and password). Each user works and stores information online. Every user's information is secure. Two users can easily exchange information with one another. The model works very well for a large community of users. It is most effective in rolling out a common technology rapidly for a community of users. It also can make the technology cheaper by exploiting economies of scale if the community of users is large.

The "SWIFT Model"

Under the "SWIFT model," technology is deployed using common industry standards, as sophisticated industries such as banking do. According to this model, each user has a computer and an application, which may be common or different across users. The user saves all work on the hard drive of the computer. No two users are able to look at each other's work. However, all users agree upon a common industry standard by which they exchange information with one another. For example, in banking, all banks agree upon a standard message format, such as SWIFT, under which they exchange information, transfer money to one another, and do a host of other services. The model allows each user to work independently but facilitates a large community of users to easily exchange information with one another. However, the model requires a community of users who are highly sophisticated and recognize the need to come together and agree upon a common industry standard. Practically, developing such a common standard and deploying it across an industry requires many years.

In the case of the microfinance industry of Bangladesh, the Microsoft Office model is what is mostly in practice today. Each MFI has its own computer and its own management information system (MIS) application. Each MFI stores information on its own. No two MFIs exchange information with one another on a frequent basis. Even the head offices and branch offices exchange information on a less-than-regular basis, often sending Excel spreadsheets by e-mail.

The SWIFT model could be very useful for Bangladesh's microfinance industry. Developing a common industry standard for exchanging information, however, is difficult to bring about in a short amount of time, as it requires a great degree of sophistication and coordination on the part of the entire microfinance industry. Even if an industry standard could be realized, it still does not address the issues of capital and capacity to introduce technology across the microfinance industry of Bangladesh.

A variation of the Gmail model is what is proposed in this report for the microfinance industry of Bangladesh. The model is most useful in rapidly deploying technology across the microfinance industry of Bangladesh and in achieving low costs due to economies of scale. For the case of Bangladesh, the Gmail model would be modified such that the centralized ICT platform serves multiple stakeholders in Bangladesh but still caters to the individual needs of each stakeholder. The model also would be modified such that the centralized ICT platform charges a fee for providing technology services to MFIs.

The Building Blocks

For a centralized ICT platform for the microfinance industry to be developed, technology changes are needed in three parts of the industry: (1) the center, where the host institution resides and provides technology as a service to all MFIs; (2) the edge, where the MFIs reside and act as the main users of technology for their daily operations; and (3) the field, where the loan officers operate and act as a branchless bank with the use of technology. Figure 6.1 illustrates the building blocks required from a technology standpoint for each part of the microfinance industry.

The Center

The institution at the center hosts all the technology and provides it as a service for a fee to MFIs. Several building blocks are required at the center:

- *Core microfinance software.* The core microfinance software serves as the minimal form of MIS required by MFIs to do their daily operations. The core microfinance software allows MFIs to run transactions, manage clients, manage human resources, do accounting, and perform related functions.
- *Core database.* A common database must be capable of storing all data from all MFIs throughout Bangladesh. The data from each institution is held securely and separately. No two MFIs can look at each other's data. MFIs can, however, agree to allow other stakeholders to see part of the information when it facilitates credit reporting, standardized reporting, and related activities.

Figure 6.1   Building Blocks for a Centralized ICT Platform

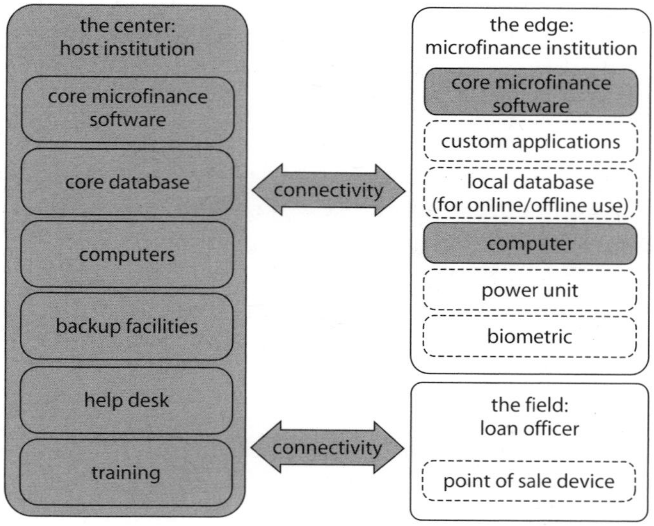

Source: Authors.

- *Computers.* The host institution uses a data center where all computer servers and physical equipment reside.
- *Backup facilities.* The data center used by the host institution also provides backup facilities in case any information is lost by accident and needs to be recovered.
- *Help desk.* The host institution operates a round-the-clock help desk that users can call to ask technical questions in case they face any difficulty using the centralized ICT platform.
- *Training.* The host institution provides training to help industry stakeholders use the centralized ICT platform.

The Edge

The MFIs serve as the edge of the centralized ICT platform. Each head office, regional office, and branch office requires a basic computing facility in order to connect to the center and do their daily operations. Some building blocks at the MFIs are optional whereas others are necessary. Following are the building blocks required for each office of an MFI:

- *Core microfinance software.* The MFI requires the capability to access the core microfinance software provided by the center. The capability may exist in form of a local application residing on a local computer or an application accessible online using a standard browser. The core microfinance software serves as the basic utility that staff at the head office, regional office, and branch office use to do their daily operations.

- *Computers.* Each head office, regional office, or branch office requires at least one computer per office to be able to do its daily operations.

- *Connectivity.* Each head office, regional office, or branch office requires the capability to connect to the center using an Internet or mobile phone network data services connection.

- *Custom applications (optional).* MFIs may choose to develop their own custom applications or buy applications from external vendors. Custom applications may allow MFIs to provide, for example, insurance products, remittance products, mobile banking services, or related applications.

- *Local database (optional, for online/offline use).* Some MFIs do not have a reliable, always-on connection to the Internet. They may want to temporarily store transactional information as it occurs while the Internet connection is not available and synchronize it to the center once the Internet connection becomes available. The local database would thus be used not as a full database but rather as a local cache for temporarily holding information.

- *Power unit (optional)*. Some MFIs do not have reliable supply of electrical power. They may use an optional power unit, such as a diesel generator or a battery-equipped solar power unit, to run the local computer.

- *Biometric devices (optional)*. MFIs that serve customers who do not have official identity cards or who are not able to sign their names may want to use biometric devices to uniquely identify customers.

The Field

MFIs may wish to operate branchless banking and equip their loan officers with hand-held devices to conduct the full suite of microfinance services. The building blocks required to facilitate branchless banking include the following:

- *Point-of-sale (POS) device (optional)*. Loan officers may use a hand-held, POS device to connect to the center and run transactions. POS devices are by powered by a rechargeable battery.
- *Connectivity for POS (optional)*. A POS device requires connection to a mobile network or a WiFi network in order to interface with the centralized ICT platform.

Basic Capabilities

The centralized ICT platform should demonstrate a set of basic capabilities in order to properly serve the microfinance industry of Bangladesh.

Scalability

The centralized ICT platform should be capable of serving the entire microfinance market of Bangladesh. The platform may be designed to initially serve only a handful of MFIs and gradually scale up to include the entire industry over several years.

Affordability

One of the main value propositions of the central platform is that it would provide technology as a service to MFIs at a low cost. The low cost can be achieved through economies of scale. The development and maintenance of the platform should thus be efficient so that affordability is not jeopardized.

Data Security

Because the platform would hold all the data of MFIs, it must offer guaranteed data security to participating MFIs. Security implies that the data should be exchanged and guarded with the most sophisticated encryption methods. It also implies that, except in certain circumstances as agreed in advance, no institution other than the owner of the data should have the authority to view the data. MFIs may agree to reveal some of their data to other industry stakeholders to allow credit checks of customers, standardized reporting, and functions beneficial to the industry. Any such agreement should be based on a signed memorandum of understanding signed between respective parties.

Innovation

The platform should have the capability to allow MFIs to rapidly roll out new products and services, such as mobile banking, credit bureaus, and electronic remittances. The platform should thus support innovation—both in terms of technology, so that the platform can adapt to the future needs of the microfinance industry, and in terms of product and service offerings, so that MFIs derive a value-added benefit from being able to offer a broad variety of products and services with less effort.

Availability

The centralized ICT platform should be available to any MFI in Bangladesh regardless of the institution's size or geographical location.

Catering to Multiple Users

Because the centralized ICT platform acts as the center that connects all industry stakeholders, it must serve a broad variety of institutions. Each stakeholder requires its own interface (or online window) through which it can access selected information within the platform. Possible interfaces for the different stakeholders are illustrated in figure 6.2.

Figure 6.2   The Centralized ICT Platform and Multiple Users

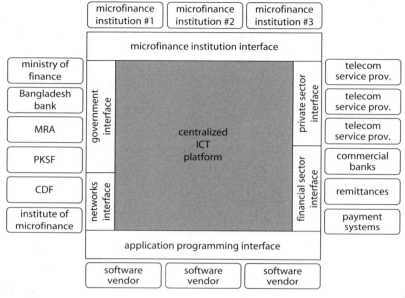

Source: Authors.

Each interface requires a memorandum of understanding between the entity using the interface and the MFI providing the data. The memorandum of understanding should safeguard the information stored by MFIs within the centralized ICT platform.

Once set up, the interface provides different stakeholders a snapshot of the microfinance market in Bangladesh at any given instance in time. For example, the government interface may allow the Bangladesh Bank to see online consolidated information, such as number of clients and outstanding loans, for the entire microfinance industry.

Adapting to Individual Needs

The centralized ICT platform should be able to provide customized services to individual MFIs throughout Bangladesh. MFIs with a simple product portfolio and a small customer base may want to use only the basic services offered by the centralized ICT platform, while MFIs with a larger suite of financial products and services and a larger customer base may want to use specialized applications to serve a diverse population of clients.

The centralized ICT platform should allow the IT staff of MFIs to develop specialized applications for the MFI they work for. Alternatively, external software vendors should be able to develop specialized applications that work with the centralized ICT platform and can be sold to individual MFIs in Bangladesh. Such a facility would allow the centralized ICT platform to meet the individual needs of MFIs throughout Bangladesh.

The flexibility to develop new applications beyond what the centralized ICT platform offers can be made possible by an "application programming interface." The application programming interface would provide the hooks with which new applications can be added to the centralized ICT platform. Figure 6.3 illustrates the availability of the application programming interface and the resulting specialized applications for individual MFIs.

Connecting to the Platform

One of the main capabilities of the centralized ICT platform is that it would allow a head office, regional office, branch office, or loan officer of an MFI to connect to the center. A connection to the center could be made using the Internet or data services offered by mobile phone networks. In fact, connectivity presents a cost and a possible constraint in

Figure 6.3   Application Programming Interface

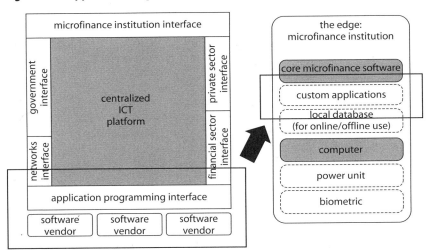

Source: Authors.

using the centralized ICT platform and is an important consideration in the design of the platform.

From the standpoint of technology, the centralized ICT platform should be designed in such a way that it meets the requirements of the less than robust communications network of Bangladesh. The platform has to operate under the regulatory environment of Bangladesh and rely upon the communications infrastructure currently available in Bangladesh. Several options exist for connecting MFIs to the centralized ICT platform.

Broadband Internet

Broadband services in the form of a digital subscriber line (DSL) could be used to connect to the centralized ICT platform. Though broadband presents the most efficient way to connect to the center and use its technology services offered, broadband services are limited in Bangladesh and are largely available only in urban areas. The cost of using broadband is also high in Bangladesh. Currently, only the state-owned incumbent operator, along with several Internet service providers, offer broadband services in Bangladesh.

Dial-up Internet

Dial-up Internet over fixed telephone lines is a second method by which MFIs could connect to the centralized ICT platform. Fixed-line telephones are available throughout Bangladesh, including in rural areas. Fixed-line coverage, however, has grown slowly and has been outpaced by mobile telephones, and the quality of service varies between urban and rural areas. Dial-up Internet is available only for the parts of the fixed-line network that have been modernized in recent years.

Data Services over Mobile Phone

Data services over mobile phone networks is still another way that MFIs could connect to the centralized ICT platform. The six mobile phone operators currently active in Bangladesh offer widespread coverage throughout the country (to roughly 40 million subscribers), including in urban and rural areas, and all six mobile operators offer Internet data services over their mobile networks. Some areas lack coverage, notably the Chittagong Hill Tracts area and the southeastern part of the country. The quality of data services also varies between urban and rural areas.

Satellite Internet

A final method by which to connect to the centralized ICT platform, particularly in areas where other Internet connectivity is not readily available, is satellite Internet. The benefit of satellite Internet is that it can be readily installed in rural and remote areas. Service providers are available that can set up satellite connectivity in rural or remote areas where Internet connectivity is not possible. Satellite Internet connections, however, are very expensive and can be justified only in places where there is a critical mass of MFIs.

CHAPTER 7

Institutional Design

This chapter describes the various models that could be followed in order to develop the institution that needs to be in place to govern and implement the centralized ICT platform. The various models are evaluated against a set of principles to provide recommendations on the approach that maps best to those principles. Additional details on the recommended approach are also provided.

Institutional Purpose and Principles

An institution is required to provide governance and support to the centralized ICT platform. As identified in figure 7.1, a number of functional and operational roles need to be developed around the platform. These include governance, microfinance engagement, technology hosting, and regulations.

A governance role is important for ensuring that the effort toward creating and implementing a centralized ICT platform is well received by participating organizations and to ensure that there is sound fiduciary accountability across all aspects of the platform. To ensure microfinance institution (MFI) engagement, it is important to establish shared cost models in order to generate market demand. A hosting and service role is

Figure 7.1   Functional and Operational Aspects of the Host Institution

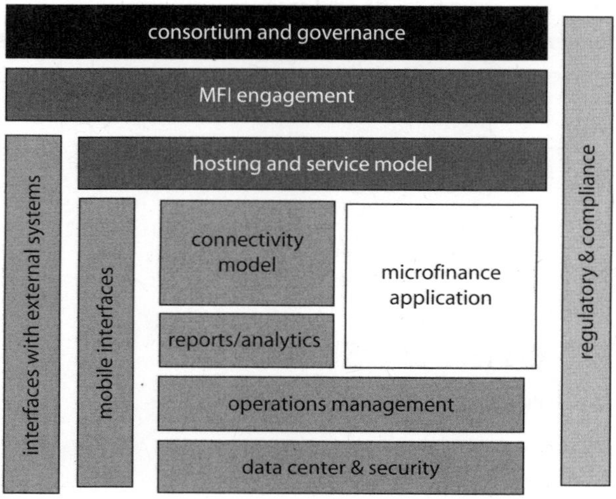

Source: Authors.

required to manage the technical aspects of the platform—from the applications to the connectivity and from the data center to security, including reports and operational aspects. The institution also needs to interface with external systems to establish connections to other enabling applications, such as mobile banking, credit bureaus, and remittances. A compliance role is also required to ensure the effort remains in adherence with all existing and evolving regulations.

A set of principles that guide the formation of the implementing institution should be established as a first step in considering the organizational approach (Hock and Senge 2005). From interviews with stakeholders, several guiding principles have emerged:

- *The implementing agency should be respected* by government authorities, the participants, and stakeholders in Bangladesh's microfinance industry to establish trust that the data of participating MFIs will be held in confidence.
- *The implementing agency should be a neutral player* in the microfinance market, independent of any financial institution or technology vendor and acting as a body focused on the overall industry rather than institutional objectives.
- *The implementing agency should be representative,* allowing and encouraging the participation of all categories of MFIs irrespective of size.

- *The implementing agency should be capable of managing* participants and the technology development and implementation process.
- *The implementing agency should be efficient in its business and costing practices*, thus ensuring that all interested parties have the capacity and capability to pay fees and purchase services.
- *The implementing agency should have a business plan that will lead it to financial sustainability*, thus ensuring its ability to deliver services to its customers.
- *The implementing agency should be financially accountable and transparent* to all participants and should establish rules for annual reporting and transparent operations.

Institutional Approaches

In Bangladesh, several institutional models could potentially be used to host a centralized ICT platform. However, when the institutional forms were considered individually using the guiding principles above, they were all found wanting. Each model has advantages and disadvantages.

Public Sector Model

Under a public sector model, a government body or some other public entity in Bangladesh would establish the requirements for the platform, would contract with technology vendors, and would provide governance and oversight for the project. Once implemented, the public agency would provide services to MFIs and other market makers.

A government agency could establish a regulatory framework that forces financial institutions to participate in the platform. This approach was taken by the government of Ghana in an attempt to implement a nationwide point-of-sale (POS) latform when it signed a $32 million agreement with technology provider Net1 UEPS Technologies for the service (du Toit 2008). The president of Ghana and the central bank have made it compulsory for the 169 commercial banks, savings and loans providers, and community banks in the country to become part of the initiative. In this circumstance, the government of Ghana absorbed the cost of implementing the solution. The model was also followed in Mexico under the Bansefi project, although Bansefi was a development bank rather than a regulatory agency. The original idea was that the government of Mexico would invest in infrastructure and, once the platform was self-sustaining, sell it to the MFIs and other stakeholders. The plan did not work well, however, due to the fact that the MFIs did not take much interest in the project because they did not invest any money in it upfront. Rather, they were all waiting to see if the project would work.

To achieve its purposes under a public sector model, the government of Bangladesh could quickly approve the platform and either establish a new entity or empower an existing public entity to become the implementing agency. Whichever approach is undertaken, the government would likely provide funding for the project, either on its own or in conjunction with other funding agencies.

Private Sector Model

Under a private sector model, a privately held company would establish the centralized ICT platform in Bangladesh. Examples from other countries suggest that this entity would be either a commercial bank or a technology company.

Commercial bank model. When a large financial institution drives this process, participation is generally limited to institutions the founding partner targets for inclusion. Initial members set all financial conditions, including the cost of participation, as well as charges that will be levied by each of the participants to each other and to their customers. Since the initial participants are usually large banks, the conditions set are generally conducive to their business needs.

According to interviews with Mercy Corps and the International Finance Corporation (IFC), Mercy Corps is implementing a commercial bank model in Indonesia. Known as the "bank of banks," this project will establish a new bank to provide wholesale loans to MFIs and other small financial institutions in Indonesia. As part of its offering, the bank of banks will develop a centralized information and communication technology (ICT) platform that it will use to manage the data of the participating MFIs. Decisions about cost structure and participation will also be made by the bank of banks.

The private sector model requires a large financial institution and a largely untapped market for success. Financial sustainability is a core requirement for a commercial bank to undertake such an effort.

Technology company model. In this scenario, a technology company would either emerge within Bangladesh or an international company would provide the central platform as a service to MFIs. The technology company would assume the cost of developing, implementing, and supporting the service. In addition, the company would underwrite the cost of promoting, selling, and marketing its solution to potential customers. Players in the market would choose to participate based on cost and effectiveness of services.

Due to their business motives, technology companies would seek profits in their involvement in such a model. In targeting the microfinance industry, one way technology companies seek profitability is to establish themselves in large markets. In cases where microfinance customers are not yielding positive returns, these companies may need to shift their business objectives to more lucrative clientele. IBM, for example, is engaged in the development of a platform for the Latin American microfinance market, where estimates for 2007 indicate that more than 600 institutions are serving more than 8 million clients and providing more than $8.6 billion in credit.[1] FINO (Financial Information Network & Operations Ltd), an India-based technology company incorporated in 2006, originally targeted microfinance clients. The company has expanded its range of clients, however, and is now serving the banking, microfinance, insurance, and government sectors.

This business-driven approach would ensure efficiency and match-to-market requirements in the centralized ICT platform in Bangladesh. Success depends on the level of market participation at prices that make the solution sustainable within a relatively short time period.

Public-Private Partnership
A public-private partnership (PPP) model assumes joint participation by a number of stakeholders interested in advancing the microfinance market. Under this model, participants would either create a new legal entity or establish a new division under an existing entity to serve as the implementing agency for the platform.

PPP: existing entity. In this model, potential users of the platform would partner with an existing public or private entity in the microfinance sector to create a new division that would become the implementing agency. Governance would be provided by the chief executive officer (CEO) and board of directors of the existing entity, and an ICT manager would be hired to manage the new division. This individual would be responsible for the operational aspects of the platform and would report to the CEO. Technology development, implementation, and support would be outsourced. To ensure that the technology solution continued to meet the needs of the microfinance industry, a technical advisory board would be formed from the potential users of and other investors in the platform.

This group would provide technical oversight on issues related to standards, data security, problem resolution, and other issues of concern to participating members. The technical advisory board would work with both the CEO and the ICT manager.

Ownership of the platform under this model would be split among users of the platform, private investors such as the technology vendor, the government, and other investors interested in supporting the microfinance sector. All of these organizations would have to make an equity investment to participate in or support the platform. Since shares would be allotted to the investors, it would be preferable if the existing entity already had a shareholding mechanism in place.

This model, while complex, benefits from its participatory nature and the ability of the potential users to select a trusted entity to serve as the neutral party of the industry.

PPP: new entity. In another take on the PPP model, potential users of the platform would jointly form a new private or public limited company that would become the implementation agency for the centralized microfinance platform. In Bangladesh, key participants could include apex organizations, MFIs, NGOs, and other microfinance stakeholders. Participating institutions would underwrite the cost of the agency and the technology development, implementation, and management.

Shareholders would establish a board of directors for governance and would hire a CEO or general manager to oversee operations. The platform could either be developed and managed within this new organization, or outsourced to a technology company.

Joint ownership of the PPP under this model would give it credibility and neutrality among the initial equity investors.

Analysis of Potential Approaches

To determine which of the models would be most appropriate in Bangladesh, each was evaluated against the principles described at the start of this chapter. As a reminder, the institutional agency should be respected, neutral, representative, capable, efficient, financially sustainable, and financially accountable and transparent.

Public Sector

In the context of Bangladesh, the government would not be a representative body because it could not provide shareholding to the MFIs.

From interviews with market players, it was learned that these organizations would like ownership in the platform. They also requested an opportunity to participate in the discussions related to standards, sector norms, and issues related to data sharing for credit bureaus and financial performance.

The government is best positioned to act as a facilitator rather than a direct provider of services. Facilitation involves creating an enabling environment and, if needed, supporting initiatives that can help private institutions increase access. As the implementing agency, the government would be a direct provider of services.

Private Sector

Private sector players that could be considered as candidates for establishing the platform include commercial banks and technology companies. However, as indicated below, both groups have several operational problems that disqualify them as possible hosts for platform.

Commercial banks. In Bangladesh, a commercial bank would not be viewed as a neutral entity by other players in the market. Evidence from interviews with MFIs in India conducted for this book suggest that a key reason why the FINO platform was not more readily accepted by MFIs was its perceived direct link between FINO and one bank in India, ICICI Bank. In addition, a commercial bank functioning as the implementing agency would not be representative of the entire microfinance industry. Since the bank's financial interests would most likely be linked to the centralized ICT platform, it is not likely that the bank would make issues related to the platform financially accountable and transparent.

Technology companies. A technology company cannot be a neutral player, representative of the industry, or transparent. Instead, the company would cater to the organizations in the microfinance market that would be willing and able to purchase its services. If not all players chose to participate in or were able to afford the central platform created by a technology company, the current fragmentation in the market would remain.

Due to the nature of its business, a technology company needs a financially sustainable business model to function as the implementing agency of a central platform. If profitability and growth goals are not being met, the company might drift away from its original mission to provide a service to the microfinance industry.

Based on the financial costs provided in chapter 8 and the costing tables A.1 and A.2 in appendix, the current stakeholders in Bangladesh are not likely to be able to cover the cost of the platform without some form of subsidy. This scenario makes it unlikely, then, that a private technology company would enter the market on its own to provide this solution. It is more probable that a technology company would enter the market as one of the partners in a public-private partnership.

Public-Private Partnership

Interviews with market players suggest that public-private partnership (PPP) is the preferred model for creation of a central MFI technology platform in Bangladesh. MFIs and apex organizations told consultants working on this book that they would be willing to participate in a PPP, that they would be interested in purchasing shares of the agency, and that they would be willing to pay for services.

PPP: existing entity. An existing entity would already be familiar to microfinance participants in Bangladesh, and the principles of respect, trust, neutrality, and transparency would have already been established among the parties.

The largest challenge with this model would be to identify a neutral, respected institution in Bangladesh with the expertise to run a large-scale technology implementation. The other challenge would be to ensure that the platform was aligned with the mission of the existing institution, as the scale of the platform could easily dwarf the existing activities and initiatives of the entity. This could create both a conflict of interest and confusion about the true role and priorities of the entity. If such an organization could be found in Bangladesh, important elements for its success would be creation of a business plan that ensured financial sustainability and the hiring of extremely competent management to handle all technical and training aspects of the platform. The CEO of the existing entity would be responsible for relationship management.

Another challenge of this model would be to ensure that all the players in the market feel comfortable aligning behind the existing entity.

PPP: new entity. Since the institutional agency would be newly formed, it would have to establish offices and hire management. One of the most important success factors in creating a new entity would be identifying and hiring the organization's CEO. This person would need to either be already well respected in the microfinance community or be able to garner respect quickly. In addition, this individual would have to be highly competent at managing this complex organization. That competency includes prior experience running a large, complex technology system. The CEO would also need to have enough knowledge of the requirements of such a system to be able to hire highly skilled and appropriate ICT experts and trainers.

Since there are many unknowns, developing a new organization involves a level of risk and uncertainty, particularly around the areas of neutrality, trust, and competence described above.

Recommended Approach

Based on the analysis of each of the models presented above and feedback from the market, a new-entity PPP appears to be the best model for Bangladesh. The primary reason this model is preferable to the existing-entity PPP model is the fact that discussions in Bangladesh did not point to any current organization that all players were willing to embrace. The following section provides more details about the way a new-entity PPP model might evolve in Bangladesh.

Organizational Model

The proposed institutional agency could be organized according to the model shown in figure 7.2.

Figure 7.2   Organizational Model

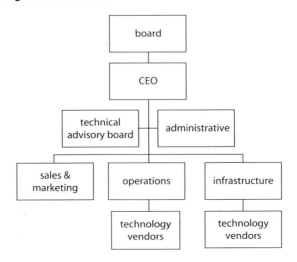

Source: Authors.

Roles and Responsibilities

MFIs that chose to use the platform would become members of the institutional agency. Membership would be obtained by purchasing shares in the agency. Members would also pay annual dues to cover operational costs. Members might also be required to pay transaction and implementation fees. The cost of entry, annual payments, and other fees would be set by all shareholders and would be approved by the board of directors.

The board of directors would provide governance and oversight of the platform. It would also have fiduciary responsibility. The board would be composed of major stakeholders and funders of the institutional agency, and members of the board of directors would not be allowed to simultaneously participate in the technical advisory board. Board members would have term limits and be guided by the agency's by-laws.

The CEO would champion the PPP's efforts. This individual would be responsible for ensuring success of all aspects of development; implementation; delivery of services; and integration with external systems, MFI participation, and compliance. A key element of the CEO's efforts would be to ensure that the majority of MFIs in Bangladesh participate in the platform. The CEO would also be responsible for the operational success of the platform.

The sales and marketing director would identify potential clients, develop sales strategies for products and services, devise commercial strategy and planning, define prices, manage customer relationships, identify new products and services, and administer service-level agreements.

The operations director would be the main contact with the software developer and coordinate the outsourced implementation teams. The operations director would be in charge of new product development in the systems and would implement diagnostics and prices, data migration, detection and fixing of errors, system design, system improvements, and MFIs' implementation processes. The director also would be responsible for continuity of the operations.

The infrastructure director would be responsible for the technical success of the platform but would also have responsibility for liaising with the technical advisory board. The infrastructure director would lead the effort to develop functional specifications, identify technology vendors, oversee product development and implementation, and provide ongoing oversight and management of the technology vendors. The director would also manage relationships with the data center vendor, telecommunications companies, hardware suppliers, MFI systems staff, and business continuity personnel. Finally, the director would finalize service-level agreements with the MFIs and ensure the viability of the disaster recovery plan.

The administrative section would be in charge of billing and collection processes, general services, general ledger, payroll administration, treasury, accounts payable, and related functions.

The technical advisory board would provide technical oversight of the platform. Members of the technical advisory board would be elected from among the users of the platform and would have a limited term. A set of guidelines would be developed to define the board's roles and responsibilities. In general, this group would ensure that the requirements of platform users are taken into consideration. These requirements would include matters related to technology requirements, vendor selection, standards, data security, training, call centers, development priorities, and pricing structures. Technical advisory board members would also be called upon to provide guidance and decision making on broad issues that affect users of the platform. Members of the technical advisory board would serve on a voluntary basis for the purpose of further developing the microfinance industry in Bangladesh.

A technology vendor or group of vendors would either be shareholders in the agency or be hired on an outsourced basis. These vendors would be responsible for all technical components of the platform: application development and support, connectivity, networking, data hosting, backup, disaster recovery, configuration, deployment, installation, training of trainers, and system support. Vendors could also be hired to provide customer support services such as ongoing training and call centers.

Note

1. Microfinance Gateway. June 14, 2008. http://www.microfinancegateway.org/p/site/m/template.rc/1.9.26179

CHAPTER 8

Cost Projections

This chapter looks into the costing of a centralized ICT platform. Though projections given here are intended to estimate the cost of the platform, the eventual cost might be lower or higher and should be refined in a detailed feasibility study to reflect the situation on the ground. The cost will also depend on the number of institutions that sign up and how long data migration might take. At the moment, some institutions claim to have some level of computerization. As the establishment of the platform commences, it might be discovered that the type of computerization capability thought to be prevalent is not at the expected level and therefore costs more than might be incurred to rectify such situations. On the other hand, there might be more institutions with the right levels, which would reduce the costs. International experience, however, shows that costs are normally more than expected when on-boarding the institutions, especially with relation to data integrity and migration.

How much will it cost to develop and maintain a centralized ICT platform for the microfinance market of Bangladesh? The economies of scale related to cost when all technology resources of microfinance institutions (MFIs) in Bangladesh are pooled in one place is one of the main reasons a centralized ICT platform is attractive. This chapter presents a preliminary financial plan based on a simple financial model and a set of underlying assumptions related to developing a centralized ICT platform in Bangladesh.

In order to develop the platform, a detailed business plan needs to be prepared for the host institution. The business plan would examine areas such as the organizational structure, mission statement, corporate strategy, revenue and expense structure, sales and marketing strategy, human resources plan, and an implementation plan needed for the institution to come into existence. It would also include an economic analysis that would measure the socioeconomic benefits beyond the financial projections.

The Methodology

The financial model used to estimate the cost of the centralized ICT platform takes into account the revenues and expenses of the host institution serving the MFIs of Bangladesh. Revenues are based on a fee that the host institution charges the MFIs in return for providing technology services. Expenses are the sum of capital expenses required to set up the host institution and the centralized ICT platform and operating expenses required to run the operations. The difference between revenues and expenses gives the financing gap. Various financing options would need to be explored to fill the financing gap and bring about the centralized ICT platform in Bangladesh.

The model assumes a three-phase implementation strategy spread over nine years. Each phase consists of three years. Ten percent of the microfinance market is served by the end of the first phase, 50 percent by the end of the second phase, and 100 percent by the completion of the third phase. The microfinance market served is taken to be the number of MFIs operating during any given year.

All estimates are based on the five-year historical growth rates of the microfinance market of Bangladesh, as shown in table A.1 in appendix. Growth rates include those of head offices, regional offices, branch offices, loan officers, customers, and loan portfolios. All estimates assume an organic growth rate, suggesting that the use of technology has no effect on the microfinance market in Bangladesh. In fact, the use of technology can accelerate the rate at which MFIs grow and expand and the rate at which the client base and loan portfolio grow. The financial case for developing a centralized ICT platform could be even more favorable if an inorganic growth rate were to be assumed, taking into account the use of technology.

To keep the projections simple, the financial model does not take into account the cost of running a help desk, a call center, or a training facility by the host institution. The model also does not take into account the cost and benefit of software customization or specialized applications that MFIs may require for using the centralized ICT platform.

The Assumptions

Given the Bangladesh microfinance market and the data obtained during the study, the following assumptions were made to set up the financial model and estimate the cost of the centralized ICT platform:

- *Time horizon.* The entire microfinance market of Bangladesh is expected to be served within a time horizon of nine years.
- *Inflation rate.* An inflation rate of 5 percent is assumed over the time horizon.
- *Exchange rate.* An exchange rate of Tk 68.03 to $1 is assumed over the time horizon.
- *Growth rate of microfinance institutions.* The number of MFIs in Bangladesh is assumed to grow at a rate of 1 percent per year over the time horizon.
- *Growth rate of head offices.* The average number of head offices per MFI is assumed to grow at a rate of 1 percent per year over the time horizon.
- *Growth rate of regional offices.* No regional offices are assumed to exist at the moment over the time horizon.
- *Growth rate of branch offices.* The average number of branch offices per MFI is assumed to grow at a rate of 16 percent per year over the time horizon.
- *Growth rate of loan officers.* The average number of loan officers per MFI is assumed to grow at a rate of 17 percent per year over the time horizon.
- *Growth rate of customers.* The average number of customers per MFI is assumed to grow at a rate of 14 percent per year over the time horizon.
- *Growth rate of loan portfolio.* The average loan portfolio per MFI is assumed to grow at a rate of 25 percent per year over the time horizon.
- *Operating expenses.* Average operating expenses are assumed to be 12 percent of the loan portfolio of each MFI over the time horizon.
- *IT expenses.* MFIs are assumed to spend on average 8 percent of their operating expenses on information technology. The model assumes that the 8 percent is paid by the MFIs as a fee to the host institution

for technology services they would use. The 8 percent forms the revenue stream of the host institution.

- *Head offices.* All head offices of each MFI are assumed to be located in urban areas; to have electric power and thus not to require power units to run computers; to have access to broadband Internet, dial-up Internet, and mobile Internet (and prefer to use broadband Internet); and no head office is assumed to requires biometric devices, since most of the transactional work is done in the field.
- *Branch offices.* Thirty percent of branch offices of each MFI are assumed to be located in urban areas, and 70 percent in rural areas; 10 percent of branch offices in rural areas are assumed to have no power and thus require power units to run computers; 30 percent of the branch offices are assumed to have broadband Internet, 23 percent to have dial-up Internet, 23 percent to have mobile Internet, and 23 percent to have no Internet connection; 10 percent of the branch offices that do not have Internet are assumed to be in an area where a critical mass of MFIs exists (as a result, these branch offices require satellite Internet); and 33 percent of the branch offices are assumed to require biometric devices.
- *Loan officers.* Twenty percent of loan officers of each MFI are assumed to be located in urban areas, and the remaining 80 percent in rural areas; 33 percent of loan officers are assumed to be in rural areas that have access to mobile Internet; 50 percent are assumed to be in rural areas with the ability to use mobile Internet to complete point-of-sale (POS) transactions and facilitate a branchless bank.
- *Host institution.* The host institution is assumed to be staffed with 67 employees, consisting of 1 CEO, 5 advisory board members, 5 vice presidents, 10 managers, technical staff, and support staff.

The Cost

Based on the financial model and assumptions given above, the cost for setting up the centralized ICT platform is estimated to be $26.18 million as shown in table A.2 in appendix. Of the total cost, $8.78 million is needed during the first three years and $17.40 million during the second three years, while $87.15 million is expected to be recovered during the last three years of implementation. Figure 8.1 sums up these financial projections.

It is expected that the centralized ICT platform will exploit economies of scale and will become financially viable by catering to the entire

Figure 8.1   Financing Requirements for the Centralized ICT Platform

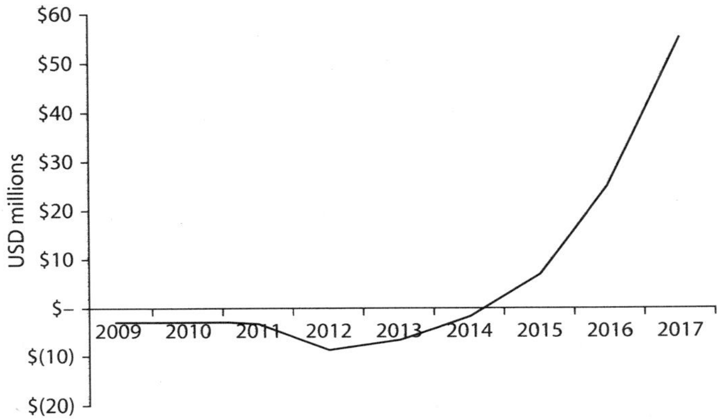

Source: Authors.

microfinance market of Bangladesh. The large financial recovery during the final three years of implementation indicates that the host institution is capable of recovering its initial investment if it sustains its operations over the long run.

Sensitivity Analysis

A sensitivity analysis was performed to determine the effects of several assumptions on the financial model described above. Four scenarios were evaluated: (1) slow implementation phasing; (2) lower expenditures by MFIs on information technology (IT) during earlier years than later years of implementation; (3) higher-than-expected per-unit costs of the basic building blocks used to set up the centralized ICT platform for the host institution; and (4) slow growth of the loan portfolios of MFIs. Each scenario is evaluated for its effect on financing requirements.

Scenario 1: Implementation Is Not Sensitive to Slower-than-Planned Implementation Phasing

The centralized ICT platform would be cost viable even if implementation were to be phased in slowly during earlier years (so that the market has time to adopt the platform) and faster during later years. In figure 8.2, scenario 1 illustrates "slower-than-planned implementation phasing." In this scenario, 5 percent of the market is captured by the end of phase 1 of

Figure 8.2   Sensitivity Analysis

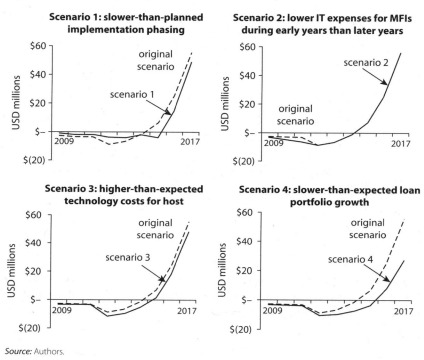

Source: Authors.

implementation, 25 percent by the end of phase 2, and 100 percent by the end of phase 3. All other assumptions are held constant according to the original scenario. The resulting cost for setting up the centralized ICT platform is found to be $15.33 million, of which $5.38 million is required during the first three years and $9.96 million during the second three years. A total of $87.15 million is recovered during the last three years.

Scenario 2: Implementation Is Not Sensitive to Low IT Expenditures by MFIs during Early Years

The centralized ICT platform would be cost viable even if MFIs were to spend less on IT during earlier years than in later years of implementation. Scenario 2 of figure 8.2 illustrates "lower IT expenses for MFIs during early years." In this scenario, participating MFIs spend 0 percent of their operating expenses on IT during the first three years, and 8 percent during remaining years. All other assumptions are held constant according to the original scenario. The resulting cost for setting up the centralized ICT platform is found to be $31.70 million, of which $14.30 million is required during the first three years and $17.40 million during the second three years. A total of $87.15 million is recovered during the last three years.

Scenario 3: Implementation Is Not Sensitive to Higher Per-Unit Costs for Setup of a Platform by the Host Institution

The centralized ICT platform would be cost viable even if the host institution faces higher-than-expected per-unit costs for the building blocks it uses to set up the technology platform. Scenario 3 of figure 8.2 shows "higher-than-expected technology costs for host." In this scenario, the host institution faces a 50 percent higher per-unit cost for setting up and operating the core microfinance software and core database. All other assumptions are held constant according to the original scenario. The resulting cost for setting up the centralized ICT platform is found to be $37.65 million, of which $10.52 million is required during the first three years and $27.13 million during the second three years. A total of $68.02 million is recovered during the last three years.

Scenario 4: Implementation Is Sensitive to the Loan Portfolio Growth Rate

The centralized ICT platform would be cost viable provided MFIs are able to maintain an appreciable loan portfolio growth rate over the time horizon. Scenario 4 of figure 8.2 shows "slower-than-expected loan portfolio growth." In this scenario, the average growth rate of loan portfolio of each MFI is lowered from 25 percent to 22 percent. All other assumptions are held constant according to the original scenario. The small change in growth rate, however, brings a much larger effect on overall costs. The resulting cost for setting up the centralized ICT platform is found to be $36.43 million, of which $9.36 million is required during the first three years and $27.07 million during the second three years. A total of $30.60 million is recovered during the last three years.

CHAPTER 9

Conclusions and Recommendations

Conclusions

The analysis of the microfinance market in Bangladesh presented in this book shows that introducing a centralized ICT platform would tremendously improve outreach to remote and rural areas of the country, introduce new and innovative products and services, reduce branch expansion costs, increase transparency in reporting, and facilitate the effective regulation and supervision of institutions licensed to provide microfinance services. Several emerging applications, such as branchless banking, m-banking, and electronic remittances to very remote and rural communities, could also contribute to these improvements. The extent of usage of these applications ensures that financial inclusion can be achieved for those that have not been served so far.

The recommended ICT platform can be sustained if the regulatory bodies in Bangladesh strengthen their requirements for standards and transparency among microfinance services providers, as required under the 2006 Microcredit Regulatory Authority Act. In addition to helping the Bangladesh Bank and regulatory authorities better manage key aspects of the microcredit business, the platform would also help drive microfinance providers in Bangladesh to computerize and to consider the advantages of a high-quality, standardized platform such as the one described in this book. Establishment of the platform in Bangladesh would benefit micro-finance institutions (MFIs), the government, the private sector, and the microfinance clients and their families, among others. The availability of an integrated financial system would provide the government and regula-tors with a basis by which to strategically intervene and provide support to sections of the society that need it.

Stakeholders within the microfinance industry in Bangladesh are all interested in having this platform established. As indicated in the criteria for the host institution, there is a need to have a neutral, transparent, and cred-ible party that is able to offer information and communication technology (ICT) services targeted to the microfinance industry. There are apex insti-tutions and networks that could champion this effort in Bangladesh. Ultimately, the institutions championing this effort need to ensure that the recommended centralized ICT platform and the proposed public-private partnership arrangements actually take place.

A number of microfinance institutions in Bangladesh have tried to acquire in-house management information systems (MISs), but they have proven either ineffective or too expensive. Despite the failures thus far, the findings of this study show that the stakeholders within the microfinance industry would like the ICT platform to be established and that they recognize the immense benefits that they would receive from such an intervention.

The Bangladesh Bank also welcomes the idea of a centralized ICT plat-form. Its leaders realize that with the enactment of the Microcredit Regulatory Authority Act, the regulatory authority will need on-time and online data and information about the health of the MFIs in order to reduce costs as they carry out regulatory functions. The on-time informa-tion and increased transparency that is expected to result from the imple-mentation of a centralized ICT platform will also help the Bangladesh Bank benchmark MFIs and therefore enhance the speed at which these institutions can be modernized and then integrated into the formal finan-cial sector. With better information about the financial health and actual extent of outreach of these institutions and their services, the government will be able to intervene strategically with policy initiatives that can eas-ily be translated into workable solutions on the ground. The government will also be able to utilize the extensive coverage of these institutions to fulfill portions of its own mandate, such as transparent safety net pay-ments and management.

The Institute of Microfinance, which was recently established with support from the Department for International Development (DFID), is currently trying to work with the networks and the microfinance regulatory authority to begin collecting and collating data in a professional manner and appreciates the fact that a centralized ICT platform would make this exercise much easier, as it would link the players with the users of their information, thereby enabling timely feedback.

Analysis of the policy and regulatory environment for this book was developed by examining the microfinance sector, the financial sector, and ICT regulations. No microfinance, financial sector, or ICT regulations were found to prevent the operationalization of the proposed microfinance platform. Going forward, the regulatory space would benefit from further embracing and facilitating new financial sector infrastructure through the centralized ICT platform, with the aim of achieving universal access to formal finance in Bangladesh. Recent technology spectrum license developments open promising avenues for financial services applications to reach the poor. Regulatory areas that could be addressed to leverage the microfinance platform include nonbank payment systems, consumer protection regulations, and strengthening of microfinance regulatory oversight.

Specific Recommendations

Several specific recommendations related to the development and implementation of a central microfinance ICT platform in Bangladesh came out of the analysis conducted for this book.

Identify Phases of Development
The costing of the platform was done according to a nine-year implementation period and its implementation divided into three phases of three years each. The first three years will cost $8.78 million, and the second phase will cost $17.40 million. During year six, the platform will break even and start making money. The total amount of revenue in the last three years will be $87.15 million, indicating that this is a viable proposition for microfinance stakeholders in Bangladesh. It is recommended that the platform starts with a pilot set of MFIs and on this basis create a robust plan to scale up operations of the centralized ICT platform nationally over a well-defined period of time, as has been proposed in this report.

Set Up the Operational Framework Correctly at the Start
Even though development of the central ICT platform may be done in stages, it is important to set up the overall operational framework in a

proper way from the very beginning. If the framework lacks scalability or neutrality, ramping up the platform's operations and successfully convincing MFIs to use the platform will be difficult in the long run.

Rely on Common, Off-the-Shelf Technology Solutions

Because lower cost is one of the main elements of a central ICT platform, it is important to rely on common, off-the-shelf technology components in building it. Such solutions would adhere to industry standards, provide lower costs due to economies of scale, and provide standard interfaces that would allow components from different vendors to connect with one another.

Rely on Outsourced Solutions

The institution hosting the centralized ICT platform may want to outsource technology development and operations and management in a way that allows costs to be minimized. The host institution, however, may wish to retain human resource functions that are core competencies for operating the centralized ICT platform and to outsource development and administration functions.

Establish Memorandums of Understanding for Access to Data

The security of confidential data of each MFI is an essential element of the centralized ICT platform. In order to ensure such security, MFIs must prepare memorandums of understanding with the government, the financial sector, and the private sector that allow each entity to have access to limited information that has been agreed upon. The institution hosting the centralized ICT platform must then ensure that the memorandums of understanding are strictly enforced.

Costing Tables

Table A.1   Microfinance Market of Bangladesh

	2002	2003	2004	2005	2006
Microfinance institutions	656	720	721	690	611
Head offices	656	720	721	690	611
Regional offices	N/A	N/A	N/A	N/A	N/A
Branch offices	5,130	5,642	7,807	7,518	9,049
Loan officers	42,918	45,702	59,215	65,766	79,464
Customers	9,461,729	10,647,170	11,963,407	13,941,823	16,096,180
Loan portfolio (Tk MM)	29,988	36,494	44,347	55,681	73,176

Source: Authors.
Note: N/A = not applicable.

Table A.2 Financial Requirements for the Centralized ICT Platform

Implementation phases	2009	2010	2011	2012	2013	2014	2015	2016	2017
	Phase 1: 10% in 3 years			*Phase 2: 50% in 6 years*			*Phase 3: 100% in 9 years*		
Revenue									
Total revenue from centralized ICT platform services ($ millions)	$0.67	$1.68	$3.16	$9.21	$18.10	$30.87	$51.47	$80.46	$120.73
Expenses									
Institution									
Total human resource expenses ($ millions)	$0.32	$0.33	$0.35	$0.37	$0.39	$0.41	$0.43	$0.45	$0.47
Total institutional setup expenses ($ millions)	$0.18	$0.00	$0.00	$0.00	$0.00	$0.00	$0.00	$0.00	$0.00
Total institutional ongoing expenses ($ millions)	$0.30	$0.30	$0.30	$0.30	$0.30	$0.30	$0.30	$0.30	$0.30
Technology									
Total capital expenses for host institution ($ millions)	$0.89	$1.10	$1.33	$4.94	$5.94	$7.01	$9.47	$10.85	$12.20
Total capital expenses for microfinance institutions ($ millions)	$0.77	$0.95	$1.16	$4.31	$5.20	$6.15	$8.32	$9.56	$10.76
Total capital expenses for branchless banking ($ millions)	$0.23	$0.28	$0.35	$1.31	$1.59	$1.91	$2.60	$3.02	$3.42
Total operating expenses for host institution ($ millions)	$0.09	$0.19	$0.31	$0.78	$1.32	$1.91	$2.68	$3.50	$4.33

Total operating expenses for microfinance institutions ($ millions)	$0.51	$1.11	$1.80	$4.52	$7.61	$11.04	$15.54	$20.31	$25.18
Total operating expenses for branchless banking ($ millions)	$0.17	$0.37	$0.61	$1.54	$2.62	$3.83	$5.44	$7.15	$8.93
Total expenses for centralized ICT platform services ($ millions)	$3.46	$4.64	$6.20	$18.07	$24.96	$32.55	$44.78	$55.14	$65.59
Financing gap									
Financing gap for setting up and running centralized ICT platform ($ millions)	-$2.78	-$2.96	-$3.04	-$8.86	-$6.86	-$1.68	$6.69	$25.31	$55.14
Financing gap per phase ($ millions)	-$8.78		-$17.40				$87.15		

Source: Authors.

Works Cited and Other Resources

ASA. 2006. "Annual Report 2006." ASA, Dhaka.

Bangladesh Bank. 2008. "Bangladesh Bank in Brief." http://www.bangladesh-bank
.org/aboutus/bbinb.html.

————. 2008b. "Economic Trends, Volume XXXIII." Bangladesh Bank, Dhaka.

BRAC. 2006. "BRAC Annual Report." BRAC, Dhaka.

Bridge, David, and Ignacio Mars. 2008. "Rural Connectivity Options for Microfinance Institutions: A Technical Note." CGAP, Washington, DC. http://www-wds.worldbank.org/external/default/WDSContentServer/WDSP/IB/2008/12/30/000334955_20081230043953/Rendered/PDF/470030WP0Box331calNote1Connectivity.pdf.

Caminos, Michele C., Stephen Prentice, Daryl C. Plummer, Brian Prentice, and John P. Roberts. 2007. "Asia/Pacific Gartner Symposium Keynote: IT Must Think Differently, Act Differently and Be Different to Decide Business Growth." Gartner, Stainford, CT.

CDF (Credit and Development Forum). 2006. "Microfinance Statistics, Volume 19." CDF, Dhaka.

CGAP. 2008. "Regulating Transformational Branchless Banking: Mobile Phones and Other Technology to Increase Access to Finance." Focus Note 43, CGAP, Washington, DC. http://www.microfinancegateway.com/files/46734_file_FocusNote_43.pdf.

Citigroup. 2008. "Citi Microfinance." http://www.citi.com/citigroup/microfinance/news.htm (accessed July 30, 2008).

The Daily Star. 2009. "Money Transfer by Mobile." October 6. http://www.thedailystar.net/newDesign/news-details.php?nid=108461.

du Toit, Christelle. 2008. "SA Firm Lands R243M Ghana Deal." MoneyWeb. May 15. http://www.moneyweb.co.za/mw/view/mw/en/page201650?oid=207123&sn=Detail.

EIU (Economist Intelligence Unit). 2008. "Bangladesh Country Forecast." EIU, New York.

Fenn, Jackie. 2006. "Innovation in Emerging Nations: The Disruption from the Bottom of the Pyramid." Harvard School of Business Studies Series, Gartner.

———. 2008. "Mastering the Hype Cycle: How to Choose the Right Innovation at the Right Time." Harvard School of Business Studies Series, Gartner.

FINO. 2008. "One Million Unbanked Indians Can Access Doorstep Banking through FINO Smart Card Based Technology Platform." Press Release, April 21. http://www.fino.co.in/press-release-pdf/2008/21-april-one%20million.pdf.

The Hindu Business Line. 2006. "ICICI Bank Launches New Initiative in Microfinance." July 14. http://www.thehindubusinessline.com/2006/07/14/stories/2006071404270600.htm.

Hock, Dee, and Peter M. Senge. 2005. One from Many: VISA and the Rise of Chaordic Organization. San Francisco: Berrett-Koehler.

IBM Financial Services Sector. 2007. "IBM Processing Hub for Microfinance." Public presentation. http://technology.cgap.org/technologyblog/wp-content/uploads/2008/02/processing-hub-public-121920071.pdf.

———. 2008. "IBM Processing Hub for Latin America Microfinance."

IMF (International Monetary Fund). 2008. "Bangladesh, Article IV Consultation: Concluding Statement." IMF, Washington, DC. http://www.imf.org/external/np/ms/2008/071508.htm.

Ivatury, Gautam. 2005. "Funding Microfinance Technology." Donor Brief No. 23, CGAP, Washington, DC.

———. 2006. "Using Technology to Build Inclusive Financing Systems." Focus Note No. 32, CGAP, Washington, DC.

McGee, Ken. 2006. "Emerging Business Trends. IT vendors Must Not Overlook Microcredit." Gartner. http://www3.villanova.edu/gartner/research/138800/138887/138887.html.

MicroCapital. 2007. "World Bank Makes $15 Million Microfinance Loan to Bangladesh's Palli Karma-Sahayak Foundation to Aid Rickshaw Drivers." MicroCapital, Boston, MA. http://www.microcapitalmonitor.com/cblog/index

.php?/archives/882-MICROCAPITAL-STORY-World-Bank-makes-15-
Million-Microfinance-loan-to-Bangladeshs-Palli-Karma-Sahayak-Foundation-
to-Aid-Rickshaw-Drivers.html.

Microfinance Gateway. June 14, 2008.

Microfinance Information Exchange. 2006. "The MicroBanking Bulletin." Issue
No. 13, Autumn 2006., Microfinance Information Exchange, Washington, DC.
http://www.themix.org/sites/default/files/MIX_2006_Autumn_MBB13.pdf.

———. 2008. "Microfinance Reference Data."

Microfinance Regulatory Authority (Bangladesh). 2006. "NGO-MFI in
Bangladesh, Volume III." Microcredit Regulatory Authority, Dhaka.

———. Forthcoming. "NGO-MFI in Bangladesh, Volume IV." Microcredit
Regulatory Authority, Dhaka.

Navajas, Sergio, Jonathan Conning, and Claudio Gonzales-Vega. 2003. "Lending
Technologies, Competition and Consolidation in the Market for Microfinance
in Bolivia." *Journal of International Development* 15: 747–70. http://arrow
.hunter.cuny.edu/research/papers/HunterEconWP213.pdf.

The New York Times. 2008. "Microfinance Success Sets Off a Debate in Mexico."
http://www.nytimes.com/2008/04/05/business/worldbusiness/05micro.html.

PKSF (Palli Karma-Sahayak Foundation). 2004. "Maps on Microcredit Coverage
in Upazila of Bangladesh, Dhaka." PKSF, Dhaka.

———. 2006. "PKSF Annual Report 2006." PKSF, Dhaka.

———. 2008. "PKSF: A Brief Profile." http://www.pksf-bd.org/about_pksf.html.

Rastra Bank. 2008. "Microfinancing towards Empowerment of Disadvantaged
Groups in Nepal: Innovations and Practices." Microfinance Department,
Rastra Bank, Nepal.

Reveille, Xavier. 2008. "Plenary Session on Technology in Microfinance."
Presentation at the The Sanabel's 5th Annual Conference, "Advancing Arab
Microfinance: Greater Social Impact through Inclusive Financial Services,"
Gammarth, Tunisia, May 6–8.

Standard & Poor's. 2007. "Microfinance: Taking Root in the Global Capital
Markets." http://www2.standardandpoors.com/spf/pdf/media/Microfinance
_TakingRootInTheGlobalCapitalMarkets_6_07.pdf.

Standard Chartered. "Access to Financial Services: Microfinance." http://www
.standardchartered.com/sustainability/access-to-financial-services/
microfinance/en/.

U.S. Department of State. 2007. "International Narcotic Control Strategy Report
2007." Bureau for International Narcotics and Law Enforcement Affairs, U.S.
Department of State, Washington, DC.

Wishart, Neville. 2006. "Micro-Payment Systems and Their Application to Mobile Networks." World Bank, Washington, DC. http://www.infodev.org/en/Publication.43.html.

Williams, Ian. 2008. "Global Users Take to Mobile Banking." Incisive Media Ltd. http://www.infomaticsonline.co.uk/vnunet/news/2214745/mobile-banking-rise.

World Bank. 2007. World Development Indicators Database. World Bank, Washington, DC.

————. 2008. "Draft Aide-Memoire on Supervision Mission for Central Bank Strengthening Project." World Bank, Washington, DC.

————. 2009. "Bangladesh: Second Poverty Microfinance Project Implementation Completion Report." World Bank, Washington, DC.

Index

Figures, notes, and tables are indicated by *f*, *n*, and *t*, respectively.